From Goode's World Atlas, © 1991 by Rand McNally R.L. 91-S-251

D1543459

Relief

Meters	Feet
3050	10 000
1525	5000
610	2000
305	1000
Sea Level	Sea Level
	500 Below
	5000 Sea Level
	10 000
	20 000

0 — 152.5 — 1525 — 3050 — 6100

Longitude East of Greenwich

PACIFIC OCEAN

S O V I E T   U N I O N

S I B E R I A

TURKESTAN

MONGOLIA

C H I N A

TIBET (PLATEAU OF TIBET)

GOBI (DESERT)

MANCHURIA

JAPAN

KOREA

NORTH KOREA · SOUTH KOREA

TOKYO · YOKOHAMA · OSAKA · KOBE · KYOTO · NAGOYA

SHANGHAI · PEKING (BEIJING) · TIENTSIN · TSINGTAO · NANJING · WUHAN

HONG KONG · VICTORIA · CANTON · T'AIPEI · TAIWAN (FORMOSA)

PHILIPPINES · MANILA · QUEZON CITY · LUZON · MINDANAO

SOUTH CHINA SEA · PHILIPPINE SEA

VIETNAM · HO CHI MINH CITY (Saigon) · HANOI · LAOS · KAMPUCHEA · THAILAND · BANGKOK (Krung Thep) · BURMA · RANGOON · MANDALAY

MALAYSIA · BRUNEI · SINGAPORE · Kuala Lumpur · INDONESIA · BORNEO · SUMATRA · Kuching · Kota Kinabalu

MALAY PEN. · CELEBES SEA · CELEBES

A F G H A N I S T A N · PAKISTAN · KARÁCHI · LAHORE · HINDU KUSH

I N D I A · NEW DELHI · DELHI · KANPUR · CALCUTTA · BOMBAY · MADRAS · BANGALORE · HYDERABAD · AHMADABAD · COIMBATORE · MADURAI

NEPAL · BHUTAN · BANGL. · DACCA · Patna · Varanasi · Allahabad

HIMALAYA · KATHMANDU · Lhasa

SRI LANKA (CEYLON) · Colombo

BAY OF BENGAL · ARABIAN SEA · INDIAN OCEAN

MALDIVES · LACCADIVE ISLANDS (India) · NICOBAR ISLANDS (India) · ANDAMAN ISLANDS (India)

MADRAS · WESTERN GHATS · EASTERN GHATS

CAPE COMORIN · DONDRA HEAD

NOVOSIBIRSK · SVERDLOVSK · OMSK · TOMSK · Krasnoyarsk · TASHKENT · SAMARKAND · Alma-Ata · Bukhara · Ashkhabad

KUNLUN SHAN · TIEN SHAN · TARIM BASIN · TAKLA MAKAN (DESERT) · ALTUN SHAN · TARIM

KURIL ISLANDS · SAKHALIN · HOKKAIDO · KYUSHU · SHIKOKU · HONSHU

SEA OF JAPAN · TATAR STRAIT

GREATER KHINGAN RANGE · HARBIN · CHANGCHUN · SHENYANG (MUKDEN)

HAINAN DAO · Gulf of Thailand · MALACCA STR.

Enchantment of the World

MONGOLIA

By Marlene Targ Brill

Consultant for Mongolia: Andrew C. Hess, Ph.D., Professor of Diplomacy, Fletcher School of Law and Diplomacy, Tufts University, Medford, Massachusetts

Consultant for Reading: Robert L. Hillerich, Ph.D., Visiting Professor, University of South Florida; Consultant, Pinellas County Schools, Florida

CHILDRENS PRESS ®
CHICAGO

Musicians performing folk music

Project Editor: Mary Reidy
Design: Margrit Fiddle

Library of Congress Cataloging-in-Publication Data

Brill, Marlene Targ.
    Mongolia / by Marlene Targ Brill.
        p.   cm. — (Enchantment of the world)
    Includes index.
    Summary: Describes the geography, history, culture,
industry, and people of Mongolia.
    ISBN 0-516-02605-4
    1. Mongolia—Juvenile literature. [1. Mongolia.]
I. Title. II. Series.
DS798.T37   1992   91-34172
951.7'3—dc20   CIP
                                                          AC

Picture Acknowledgments
Courtesy Department Library Services American
Museum of Natural History: Neg No 258395, 26 (center),
Neg No 410784 Original No S284, 26 (left)
AP/Wide World Photos: 8, 54 (right), 56, 57 (left), 59 (top
left), 60 (2 photos), 63, 73 (left), 89 (right)
The Bettmann Archive: 38
H. Armstrong Roberts: © Charles Phelps Cushing, 45 (left)
Historical Pictures Service: 42
North Wind Picture Archives: 39

**Ontario Science Centre, Toronto/China: 7000 Years of
Discovery:** 45 (right)
Photri: 29, 66 (left); © **Peoples Republic of China,** 108
(bottom)
Reuters/Bettmann: 59 (bottom left and right)
Root Resources: 9, 92 (right), 102 (right), 105; © **Irene E.
Hubbell,** 27 (left), 53, 103 (bottom), 104 (bottom left);
© **Jane P. Downton,** 67 (right), 95, 104 (bottom right);
© **Howard Sochurek,** 69 (left), 71 (right), 77, 83, 87 (right),
89 (left), 102 (left), 104 (top); © **L. LaFrance,** 99
© **Irene Slegt:** Cover Inset, 5, 6, 11, 15 (right), 17, 21, 22, 23,
24 (bottom left), 32, 66 (right), 67 (left), 72, 82 (right), 84,
92 (left), 94, 96 (bottom), 101 (right), 103 (top), 109
© **Eloise Smith:** 4, 10 (2 photos), 12 (2 photos), 14 (bottom
right), 65 (2 photos), 73 (right), 76, 78 (top left and right,
bottom left and right), 87 (left), 88 (2 photos), 90
(2 photos), 96 (top), 98 (left), 100, 101 (left), 123
SuperStock International, Inc.: 112; © **Dankwart von
Knobloch,** Cover, 14 (left), 98 (right); © **Holton
Collection,** 13
TSW-CLICK/Chicago: © **Alain Le Garsmeur,** 68, 108 (top)
UPI/Bettmann Newsphotos: 26 (right), 54 (left), 57 (right)
© **Lois Riley Wheeler:** 14 (top right), 15 (left), 16, 18, 24
(top and bottom right), 27 (right), 69 (right), 71 (left), 78
(center), 80 (2 photos), 82 (left and center)
Len W. Meents: Maps on 19, 43, 49, 103, 106
**Courtesy Flag Research Center, Winchester,
Massachusetts 01890:** Flag on back cover
Cover: Higland Camp Mongolian Nomads
Cover Inset: Ger style monastery in the countryside

A small forest of larch trees

TABLE OF CONTENTS

Chapter 1

THE LAND OF
THE BLUE SKY

The sky seems richer over the high plains of Mongolia. There is a sense of expansiveness far greater than the country's present Asian borders. And for good reason. The feeling has evolved among Mongols after centuries of wandering over vast Asian grasslands in search of food and water for their flocks. This constant adapting to nature produced a strong bond between the people, their animals, and especially the spacious land. Mongols call their home the "Land of the Blue Sky."

Long ago, nomadic tribes roamed Mongolia's rugged mountain ranges and colorful grasslands. To survive, the wanderers met nature's challenges by taming horses, raising livestock, and hunting with bows and arrows. As these mounted archers moved from place to place, they eventually united under one mighty leader, Genghis Khan, more than seven hundred years ago.

Under Genghis's direction, warriors swept beyond Mongolian homelands. Genghis Khan and his descendants built an empire that stretched from eastern Europe to the Pacific Ocean. The Mongol Empire became one of the largest empires in Asian history, providing a vital link between the distant cultures of Europe, the Middle East, China, and India.

Opposite page: Mountain ranges stand out against the blue sky.

In 1989 when there were still close ties between Mongolia and the Soviet Union, it was not unusual to see Soviet soldiers in Ulan Bator.

During centuries that followed, the empire crumbled. Stronger powers reclaimed their land and suppressed Mongolian warlords. Gradually, China, Tibetan Buddhism (the form of Buddhism practiced in Tibet), and then Russia influenced Mongolia's culture, politics, and economy. Today, much of that ancient empire belongs to three separate nations: Mongolia or the Mongolian People's Republic, the Soviet Union, and China.

Independence for the proud Mongols has been a constant struggle against stronger influences. Conflict continued until 1921, when Sukhe Bator led the first successful people's revolution. Mongolia became an independent people's republic three years later on November 26, 1924. However Russian-Soviet influence remained strong in all aspects of daily life for the next sixty-five years.

Throughout the spring of 1990, the people's voices rose again in protest. This time, Mongols opposed close Soviet relations.

A herder on a horse-breeding farm

Mongols chose a freer form of government with limited ties to the Soviet Union. They wanted a say in running their country and freedom to expand economic and political relations worldwide. By then, Soviet assistance had helped Mongolia begin the gradual change from an isolated country of herders to an industrial society connected by modern technology to the rest of the world. Once again, Mongols were moving on an adventure under the blue skies.

RELIGION

Official government policy discourages the practice of religion, but this is not aggressively pursued. The constitution grants equal rights for citizens, but clearly separates religion from any state or educational functions. For years Communist party propaganda discredited spiritual influences in Mongolian life. But even with restrictions, interest in religion persists.

Tibetan Buddhism, or Lamaism, provides the most attraction for Mongols currently. Former religious leaders are returning to the priesthood and younger men are ready to make lifetime religious

Above: Monks in the Gandan Monastery
Right: An altar inside a ger

commitments once again. Statues of Buddha are fairly common in most homes. Moreover, there is renewed interest in spiritual life and the role religion has played throughout Mongol history.

In a land of unlimited skies and endless steppe, ancient nomads believed heaven and earth had sacred meaning. Heaven, with its many gods, was the supreme source of power. All natural wonders below — sun, moon, stars, caves, mountains, rivers, forests, fire, air — were objects of worship.

Some early tribes regarded their rulers as "sons of Heaven," men blessed by authority from heaven to rule. Individuals with special religious abilities, called *shamans*, communicated with the gods and learned how to recognize rulers. This practice of religion, which is similar to the way in which Native North Americans practiced their religion, became known as Shamanism. It was the main religion practiced in Mongolia before Buddhism.

Worshipers spin prayer wheels at Gandan Monastery.

Shamans interpreted messages about heaven and earth. Often a shaman's primary job was to heal body and mind and call on spirits. A shaman wore colorful clothing and used chants, drums, and wild dances to reach the spirits. As he carried out his jobs, the shaman preserved tribal folklore by keeping real and imaginary tales alive.

Few shamans practice today. However, their influence remains, particularly in remote rural areas.

When Tibetan Buddhism became widespread in the sixteenth century, *lamas*, or monks, blended their faith with ancient beliefs. Horsemeat offerings before traditional Buddhist ceremonies reflected back to days when animals were sacrificed to worship ancestors. Mongolia's more ceremonial and mystical form of Buddhism was easily accepted. Soon Buddhist writings covered every important tradition of Mongolian family life. Mongols

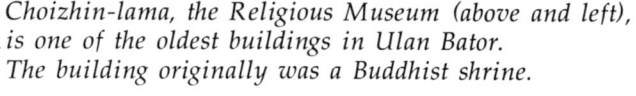

Choizhin-lama, the Religious Museum (above and left), is one of the oldest buildings in Ulan Bator. The building originally was a Buddhist shrine.

consulted lamas for weddings, funerals, new homes, and a child's first haircut, which was considered an important milestone. More recently, Mongols practice Buddhism only as it affects celebrations, holidays, and personal behavior.

Today, the government admits that there is a place for religion in modern Mongolia and recognizes its influence in the past. Choizhin-lama, the Religious Museum, displays articles used during religious ritual. The museum was once the Temple of Generous Mercy, a Buddhist shrine built between 1903 and 1905. It is one of the oldest buildings in Ulan Bator, Mongolia's capital.

In addition, the government spent considerable funds to restore the main Buddhist monastery, also in Ulan Bator. Walled Gandan

A view of Gandan Monastery from the street

Monastery, with its pagoda-roofed buildings, houses about one hundred monks. In 1971 the government permitted the monastery to reopen its religious school to educate new monks. For years, the school provided the only formal religious training in Mongolia. Government reforms during 1990 led to reopening another 40 of 470 monasteries that were forced to close.

Gandan accepts only one in five who wish to become monks. Monks with shaved heads and wearing yellow robes hold regular prayer sessions. A few young men sit behind rows of older men in the incense-smelling temple. They sit cross-legged on prayer boards chanting and fingering beads and metal bells as tourists and worshipers wander past. They are preserving the past for future generations.

Mongolian nomads (above) make their living raising livestock such as goats (top right) and camels (right).

STEPPE LIFE—THEN AND NOW

Most of Mongolia is a vast steppe, a large semidry, grass-covered plain. The Asian steppe often has been referred to as hostile land. With harsh weather, little water, and only pockets of vegetation, the steppe permitted few large settlements of people. Only twentieth-century technology allowed for growth of villages, towns, and a few modern cities.

Despite its shortcomings, the land provided excellent grazing. For centuries, tribes wandered under the blue skies seeking food for their flocks. Seemingly endless supplies of goats, camels, yaks, sheep, cattle, and especially horses provided products for basic food, clothing, and shelter. One early Russian explorer wrote, "Mongolia was a country destined by God for animal husbandry."

Livestock herding is still a major occupation today. Herding families work hard from dawn into the night tending their flocks.

A herder uses his urgha *(left) as a lasso to return a roving animal. Herders milking their horses (right)*

On a typical day, herders spend about ten hours on horseback, or more recently, jeep and motorcycle. The entire family awakens before dawn to begin their chores. Women prepare breakfast, milk the camels and goats, and clean the *gers*, or felt-covered tents. They spend the rest of the day churning butter; making cheese, yogurt, and other foods for two more meals; sewing clothes; or completing other important household projects. After breakfast the men drive the herd to pasture. Throughout the day they look for animals that wander into the far-reaching steppe. Herders use *urghas*, poles with rope loops at the end, to return roving animals to the herd. At night men bring the animals back for watering and milking. Then the family gathers for a night of rest, games, and storytelling.

Mongolian nomads have been following similar routines for centuries. However, exposure to modern technology through contact with industrialized neighboring countries has changed

Today some herders use a motorcycle or jeep in place of horses.

some of the old ways. Many people who were once nomadic
herders now raise crops with updated farm equipment. Dry desert
and steppe lands sprout grains and vegetables—thanks to modern
irrigation. As in the past, large numbers of people from the
countryside move their gers with the seasons to tend their herds.
But trucks rather than oxen often transport the homes.
Motorcycles compete with horses in some villages. And many
Mongols watch television inside their gers.

Mongolia is one of the more progressive modern countries in
Asia. Rapid change has given Mongolia two faces. On the steppe
and with older Mongols, many ancient customs persist. However,

An apartment building overlooks a ger in the yard.

the future appeals to younger generations. They see industrialization as a way to break free of traditional roles as herder and milkmaid.

New and old stand together most strikingly in Ulan Bator, Mongolia's capital and major city. High-rise apartment complexes overlook rows of gers surrounding the city. Office workers rush to work in Western dress, while herders wear traditional clothes.

Until recently, Mongolia was noted primarily for its buffer position between two political giants—the Soviet Union and China. However, the Mongolian People's Republic is reviving its heritage while educating its people for an independent role in the modern world.

Chapter 2

THE WONDERS
OF NATURE

The Mongolian People's Republic is the core of an older and larger Asian region that was once known as Mongolia. Today, Mongolia is a bowl-shaped country located in the heart of Asia. At the widest point its land stretches 790 miles (1,271 kilometers) from north to south and 1,500 miles (2,414 kilometers) from east to west. In total, Mongolia covers 604,250 square miles (1,565,000 square kilometers), an area the size of Texas, New Mexico, Arizona, Arkansas, and Louisiana in the United States.

Mongolia has no sea access. Instead, the nation shares its 2,902-mile (4,670-kilometer) southeast and southwest borders with China and its 1,866-mile (3,003-kilometer) northern border with the former Soviet Union. Mongolia's position between these two superpowers has resulted in considerable border conflict and political and economic difficulty throughout history.

MOUNTAINS AND PLATEAUS

Mongols think of their country as divided into two major zones—the Khangai in the north and the Gobi in the south. The Khangai zone has vast mountain ranges, deep valleys, salt lakes,

Opposite page: A nomad settlement is dwarfed by the landscape around it.

and elevated steppe. This larger area is where the main water sources flow and weather is more favorable. The Gobi portion of the country lacks sufficient water and has sparse dry grasslands in addition to sandy desert. There are more people, farming, and industry in the north. But Gobi vegetation supplies nutritious food for animals and the area has abundant mineral reserves. Both regions are valued for their rich, varied features. From hot springs, waterfalls, glacier boulders, volcanic depressions, and lush forests to rolling plains and shifting sand dunes, Mongolia delights the senses with a surprising assortment of colors, smells, and wondrous sights.

The northern regions of Mongolia are very mountainous. The average altitude is 5,182 feet (1,579 meters)—almost 1 mile (1.6 kilometers) above sea level. Gigantic snowcapped peaks pierce the sky from one of three main mountain ranges that cross Mongolia.

The longest and most western mountain system is the Altai. The Altai range rises in the northwest and gradually changes into rolling hills and rugged plains as it extends southeast. The range contains the only glaciers left in Mongolia. Many rivers and lakes flow from these glaciers into Central Asia and the Pacific Ocean. Their banks provide retreat for swans, pelicans, and geese, as mountain eagles soar overhead. Under water, carp, trout, salmon, and pike leap through rocky brooks. The Altai Mountains also contain the country's tallest peak. The Nayramdal Uul reaches 14,350 feet (4,374 meters) above sea level. Forested mountains offer shelter for bears and wolves who prey on the deer, elk, and other forest animals.

The second-largest mountain range, the Khangai, extends along central Mongolia almost parallel with the Altai Mountains. The

A herd of horses in the rugged Khangai Mountains

Khangai Mountains contain some of the most beautiful natural resources in the nation. In the northern Khorgo region there is a small area of about ten inactive volcanoes. Picturesque mountains surround the craters, some with peaks of 9,600 feet (2,926 meters). Cedar, larch, fir, and other evergreen trees cover the largest mountains. Inside the craters are sparkling lakes and caverns with interesting cone-shaped formations. River valleys produce pasture for farming hay. The area nearby is thick with shrubbery, rare juniper and edelweiss (an herb), and different varieties of flowers and berries. The woods are home to marmot, the country's most sought-after furbearing animal, wolves, foxes, deer, and other wild animals and birds.

On the west slope of Mount Khangai is lovely Lake Bayan. This deep national treasure comes well stocked with colorful fish and otter. Lake waters safeguard the glowing sand dunes roamed by

Lake Khubsugul reflects the surrounding mountains.

argali, Mongolia's spiral-horned wild sheep. Archaeologists retrieved remnants of cast-iron implements and large blue bricks from Lake Bayan. Popular myth states that a city once flourished here and disappeared into the depths of the lake.

Shimmering emerald Lake Khubsugul lies in another branch of the Khangai Mountains, called the Khubsugal Mountains. Huge caves along its jagged shores reveal traces of primitive life in addition to copper, zinc, gold, asbestos, and marble. Many other areas of Mongolia provide a wealth of clues to the beginning of civilization.

Between the Altai and Khangai mountains in central Mongolia lies a high plateau called the Great Lakes Basin. The region is known for its sand, fertile plains, and lakes. More than three hundred lakes snake through the basin. But they are mostly rough

Mongolians enjoying a picnic at Uvs Lake

and unsuitable for navigation. Mongolia's largest lake, Uvs Lake, is located on the plateau, covering 1,300 square miles (3,367 square kilometers).

The third major mountain range, the Khentei, is shortest and lowest. The Khentei Mountains, with peaks of 8,000 feet (2,438 meters), extend from northeast to southwest Mongolia, wrapping around the capital city of Ulan Bator. Northeast of the city the range is covered with dense pine, larch, fir, cedar, and birch trees. Within the forests are elk, deer, bear, lynx, wolves, raccoons, squirrels, and wild birds, such as grouse and partridge. The Khentei also provide vacationers with medicinal hot springs. However, as the system moves southeastward, the mountains diminish into a low grassy plateau.

Nearly 75 percent of Mongolia is treeless steppe. These vast rolling plains supply Mongols with the best pastures, hay fields, and forests. The steppe also yields one of Mongolia's most valued

The variety of Mongolia's topography includes pebbly soil on the edge of the Gobi Desert (above), vegetation growing on the flat steppe (below), and rocky mountains and woods (right).

products—the horse. Mongolian horses are smaller and sturdier than Western horses. They have large heads, shaggy coats, and stocky legs. Sturdy bodies help the horses to withstand extreme steppe temperatures and to survive on little vegetation. Horses have governed nomadic steppe life for centuries. Mongol children have always learned to ride as soon as they could walk. During Mongol conquests horses allowed swift maneuvers during combat. Wealth was measured by the number of horses a family owned. Today with more emphasis on industry and an equal supply of camels, horses play a smaller role in the economy. Still, horses are important for milk, meat, hides, fuel, and sport.

GOBI DESERT

Rolling plains run along the northern fringe of the Gobi Desert, an unusual tract of land stretching across southern Mongolia and into northern China. In Mongolia, people refer to "a gobi" rather than desert. Their term describes the flat, pebbly soil with little vegetation that covers much of the region. Only about 15 percent of the Mongolian Gobi has sand dunes as on other deserts. When they occur, dunes can rise to 1,000 feet (305 meters). Most of the Gobi is semidesert. It has some vegetation other than cactuses. The only water that can be found are springs that develop from occasional heavy rainfalls.

Other unique features of the Gobi are the colorful and unusual rock formations. Travelers as far back as Marco Polo told of magnificent Gobi stones. Black, browns, mauves, reds, oranges, and white come alive at sunrise or sunset. Roy Chapman Andrews, an American zoologist and explorer who led expeditions to the Gobi in the 1920s and 1930s, wrote, "Before us

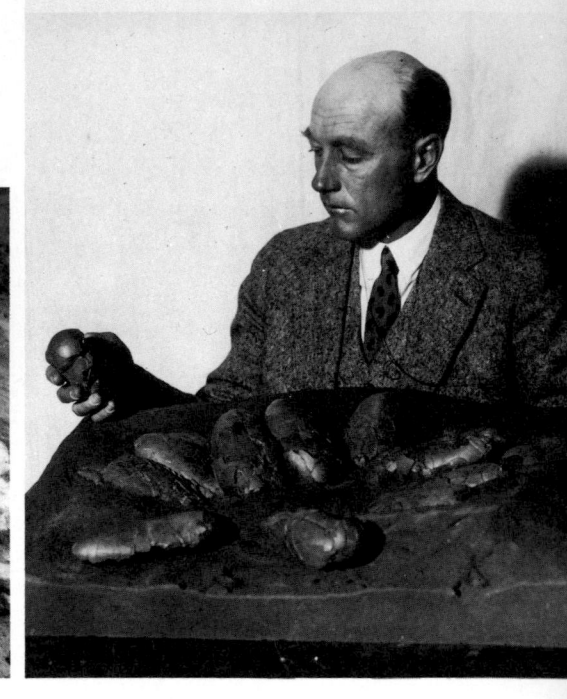

Roy Andrews and his guide, Merin, in the moonlight at Flaming Cliffs (above) where Andrews found the first Protoceratops dinosaur skull (right) Andrews, who represented the American Museum of Natural History in New York City, shows his find of dinosaur eggs (far right).

lay Mongolia, a land of painted deserts . . . a panorama so endless that we seemed to have reached the very summit of the earth."

Large volcanic, or basalt, rock formations shape much of the desert's beauty. In the eastern Gobi, giant basalt columns stand like clusters of six-sided poles. Other formations housed some of the best archaeological treasures ever found. Three small mountains in the southern Gobi called *Gov Gurvan Saikhan*, or "Three Gobi Beauties," were the discovery site of the first Protoceratops dinosaur skull. Roy Andrews located the fossil at Flaming Cliffs. His team, representing the American Museum of Natural History in New York, named the area during sunset one evening as the rocks blazed a fiery red. Mongolian-Soviet, and more recently Mongolian-American, expeditions have discovered remains linking humans to earlier forms of life.

Between these mountains, the *Yelyn Am Valley* "Valley of the Condors," furnishes rocky hideaways for birds of prey, especially

Wildflowers in Yelyn Am Valley (left) and the tough desert grass of the Gobi (right)

condors. The deep gorge allows many streams to form. Thus the valley is rich with perfumed grasses and wild sheep and goats. Some of the aroma comes from the wild onions and licorice roots growing among the tough desert grass called *gi-gi-tsao*. Mongols have many uses for this grass, including chopping it for horse feed and weaving its seven-foot (two-meter) threads into baskets, mats, brooms, and fasteners for gers. Licorice roots are pulled, sun-dried, and sold worldwide.

There is a legend about a warrior's mother who tried in vain to entice her wandering son home. The old woman begged and pleaded. When all else failed, she sent her son a batch of sweet-scented Gobi grass. The young man could not resist the smells of home and returned to his family.

The Gobi is host to many forms of wildlife. Breeders care for herds of horses, two-humped (Bactrian) camels, and cashmere goats. Sheep, antelope, yaks, gazelles, and bears roam through the semidesert regions. Huge black vultures with wingspans of 6 feet (1.8 meters) fly overhead looking for dead meat to eat. Lizards, spiders, and deadly snakes slither between the pink-blossomed saksaul plant and around tamarisks, trees that provide fuel in the desert. Older Mongols call the tamarisk *modo'en khan*, the "king of trees." The name derived from the way the tree burns with a steady blue flame. Mongols say the tree "burns without complaining and meets death like a king."

CLIMATE

The great chieftain, Genghis Khan, once called Mongolia "the place of everlasting blue skies." Indeed, the sun shines an unprecedented 250 days each year.

Slightly more water falls as snow, rather than rain, over the mountainous northern regions. Annual rainfall here varies from ten to fifteen inches (twenty-five to thirty-eight centimeters). In the Gobi region annual rainfall is usually less than five inches (twelve centimeters). When rain does fall, it is usually in the summer between July and August. Then cloudbursts are short and heavy. Threat of high water from melting snow in spring or flash floods in summer is very real.

Winters are long and cold. They run from the first snowfall in early October through the initial signs of spring in April. Winter temperatures range from 5 degrees to -22 degrees Fahrenheit (-15 degrees to -30 degrees Celsius). In January, the coldest month, temperatures can plunge as low as -50 degrees Fahrenheit (-46 degrees Celsius). Particularly harsh winters cause heavy losses as animals starve in frozen pastures. Summer temperatures average a pleasant 64 degrees Fahrenheit (18 degrees Celsius), with extremes reaching 102 degrees Fahrenheit (39 degrees Celsius).

There can be severe temperature changes within a single day.

Winters are long and cold.

Temperatures can vary as much as 55 degrees Fahrenheit
(30 degrees Celsius). These sudden changes contribute to a
buildup of strong winds. In the Gobi, powerful spring winds swirl
the shifting sand into sandstorms that can darken skies as far
away as Ulan Bator in the northeast. In the north, mighty winds
turn into hailstorms. Fierce earthquakes also plague Mongolia.
However, damage to human life is relatively limited because few
areas are densely populated.

In spite of harsh weather and uncultivated regions, Mongols
have great fondness for their homeland. Dashdorjiin Natsaghdorj,
famous nineteenth-century author acclaimed as founder of
modern Mongolian literature, wrote this verse from "My Native
Land":

> The fertile virgin-lands between Altai and Khanghai;
> Land of our eternal destiny where ancestors lie;
> Land grown mellow under the golden rays of the sun;
> Land grown eternal under the silver moon.
>
> This is my native land,
> Mongolia the beautiful!

Chapter 3

A NATION OF WANDERERS

Early Mongols believed they were descended from supernatural animal ancestors. The most popular male animal was a blue-gray wolf, and the most popular female was a doe. Traditional mythology noted that a doe and wolf once settled at a sacred mountain in northeast Mongolia. When the animals mated and gave birth to a son, Mongolia began. Mongolia's most famous leaders, such as Genghis Khan, were said to be descended from the wolf and doe. There are sites where pictures representing these ideas of ancestry were carved into cliffs. The oldest cave drawing goes back almost six hundred years.

Original Mongols were the last of a long line of conquering people who came from the north. The hardy steppe landscape nurtured their nomadic culture. Their wandering descendants became a principal force of change on the Eurasian continent between the thirteenth and fourteenth centuries. By as early as 1500 B.C., the Mongolian steppe had become the heartland of an area that fostered several major nomadic empires.

Warfare governed nomadic history from ancient times. Early Chinese chronicles recorded tales of northern horsemen who attacked their villages. Invading nomads continually overpowered neighboring fixed settlements and each other. The conquering and conquered groups absorbed bits and pieces of each other's culture. But the core of steppe life barely changed for centuries as a result of its contact with Chinese settlements.

TRIBAL POLITICS

Early steppe populations north of China were composed of groups of people who spoke variations of the Turkish language and the modern Mongol language. Families of blood relations formed clans. In turn, many clans lived together as a single tribe. Each tribe had social levels of princes, common people, and slaves who were captives from earlier conquests. Individual tribes varied in language, customs, economic need, and politics. These differences caused conflict and fighting between tribes and peace was rare.

Military might formed the basis of political activity for over two thousand years. Steppe armies were small compared with those of nearby states. Gradually the nomads who spoke Mongol began to grow in numbers. These Mongols developed superior battle tactics to withstand larger enemy forces. They relied on their abilities as horsemen and warriors rather than on numbers to survive in

Archery is popular as a sport and many Mongols are skilled with a bow and arrow.

battle. Unlimited steppe horses gave Mongols the advantage of being mobile. And their skill with bow and arrow reduced hand-to-hand combat.

Mongol history states that tribes never went into open battle unless they were assured of winning. With their nomadic life-style, Mongols easily outmaneuvered their enemies. Common military strategy was to launch a swift surprise attack with a small group. This group lured defending enemy troops into a tiring chase. When their opponents grew weary, the majority of the steppe army pounced on the unsuspecting victims. Leaders of China, Persia, and other nations complained that steppe horsemen played by their own rules. Only nomads could conquer nomads.

Tribal leaders were the best fighters and planners. Chiefs, or *khans*, also led frequent migrations for survival in the constant battle against climate and geography. However, chiefs and leaders changed with the blustery steppe winds. When a chief's military success and leadership ability declined, tribes looked to new leaders for protection.

Nomadic history was full of change; and yet certain patterns continued to repeat themselves until the eighteenth century.

First, constant conflict and shifting loyalties among neighboring tribes mingled races, language, and customs. Second, Mongol tribes raided Chinese farmers repeatedly for loot, often provoking slaughter and looting in response. Third, one conqueror occasionally absorbed many similar tribes into a larger empire.

There are few reminders of these early tribes. Their constant movement left little time to record day-by-day happenings. And many tribes were without written languages. Still, archaeologists discovered and translated stone carvings that go back to the eighth century A.D. The Orkhon Inscriptions tell the history of Turkish rule in Mongolia. They give readers some idea of how suspiciously Turks and most Mongols viewed their southern Chinese neighbors. Mongols needed farm goods from these neighbors to survive. But the inscriptions warned that nomads would be corrupted and destroyed if they became enticed into urban and farm life.

FIRST MONGOLS

Farmers and herders always had trouble existing side by side. Thus, relations between nomads and the Chinese were difficult throughout the entire history of these two peoples. Neither side totally controlled the other. There were constant wars, and treaties were made and broken. However, steppe nomads usually had the advantage.

In the third century B.C., an empire of organized tribes called the Hsiung Nu swept from the Gobi across the Yellow River to raid northern China. Chinese Emperor Shih Huang Ti of the Han Dynasty fought off the attackers and chased them mercilessly back across the desert. To prevent further invasions, the emperor built a stone barrier along the norther border of China. The Great Wall of China was thirty inches (seventy-six centimeters) thick and spanned 1,684 miles (2,710 kilometers), a distance too long to defend well. The Hsiung Nu had little difficulty returning and seizing all of northern and western China north of the Yellow River. Chinese and Hsiung Nu warriors alternated control of the land between the northern Mongolian Gobi and China's Yellow River.

After centuries of fighting, the Hsiung Nu Empire fell apart. Some tribes migrated to China. Others fanned into Europe in the fifth century and evolved into the feared Huns. When the Hsiung Nu finally ceased to threaten the Han Empire, other tribes from Mongolia took their place raiding Chinese farmlands and regulating major Asian trade routes.

By A.D. 500 another empire, the Juan, thrived on the steppe. Under their powerful leader, Toulun, the Juan drove competing tribes westward to the Caspian Sea. Toulun maintained constant fighting over a 2,000-mile (3,219-kilometer) stretch of Central Asia.

TURKISH UPRISING

Just as the Juan reached their peak, problems developed among the various groups within the empire. An uprising began in the Altai Mountains. One story suggested that fighting began after Bumin, a chief of a people related to the Mongols by language, asked to marry a Juan princess. Bumin had been a slave who worked in the iron mines. Empire leaders claimed that no Juan could marry a common "blacksmith slave." Bumin challenged the refusal with open revolt. Uprisings in this major base of Juan power split the empire. From 551 to 556, the Turks waged battle until they defeated the remaining Juan Empire. Bumin became the first Turkish emperor.

The Turks established their own empire on the central steppe where the Mongolian People's Republic is today. Then they pressed across northern and central Asia. These early Turkish conquests began a western migration into Europe that significantly changed the course of world history for the next one thousand years.

Turkish rule soon led to control over Asian trade routes. For the first time among steppe empires, trade became an important element in the economy. A barter system began for exchange of goods. Eastern Turks shipped Chinese silk west to Byzantium through Persia. Here western Turks negotiated sales. A strong relationship between trade and war developed among Turkish tribes.

Bumin's warring relatives divided the empire after his death. In the decades ahead they ordered beheadings, poisonings, and other cruel acts against fellow leaders. The Chinese took advantage of the split in leadership, as they had in the past. They played one faction against the other to cause conflict. And they joined forces with Tibetans and Arabs to weaken Turkish rule.

By the late eighth century, the only victorious Turkish tribe on the eastern steppe was the Uighurs, a group allied with the Chinese. Uighurs overthrew the few remaining Turkish leaders and established their own empire in Central Asia. Soon they controlled trade routes, exchanging horses, jade, and other valuables for Chinese silk.

As with other conquering tribes, the Uighurs adopted customs from neighboring groups, particularly the Sogdians. The Sogdians taught the Uighurs about organized religion and multistoried brick buildings with fresco paintings. They persuaded some Uighurs to learn agricultural techniques and to irrigate the desert. Equally important, Uighurs adopted Sogdian simplified script. This writing made Uighurs the first literate steppe kingdom. Even with these advances, military strength and politics still dominated steppe life.

The Uighur tribe lasted as a key force until the thirteenth century. As they weakened, other steppe tribes merged and expanded into the Middle East and Russian steppe. Chinese border empires rose to fill voids left by declining Turkish and southern Chinese empires. The end of the Turkish Empire marked the beginning of a long transition period on the steppe. This shifting ended with the formation of the greatest world empire of the time under a single leader, Genghis Khan.

THE GREAT KHAN

In 1162 a first child was born to a Borjigin Mongol chief of forty thousand tents, who sought to unify the steppe. Legend has it that the baby held a large rubylike blood clot in his hand at birth. The Mongols believed this was a sign of the boy's destiny for greatness. But no one knew that he would be so great a leader as to go far beyond his father's dream of unity and conquer much of the continent.

According to Mongol custom, the newborn son was to receive a name representing the family's most important recent event. As the tribe feasted on broiled sheep and horse meat after winning a battle, the baby's father named his son Temujin after the captured chieftain of a tribe of Turkish-speaking warriors.

Temujin had to prove himself worthy at an early age. When he was nine years old, Turks poisoned his father. The old chief's followers doubted they would be safe with a nine-year-old boy. Rather than rally around Temujin, the tribes rejected his authority and abandoned his family to die in the wilderness. But Temujin did not die. Instead he used his skills as a shrewd warrior and politician. With each brave act he gained followers. He initiated raids, treaties, and marital alliances to regain his family's position among steppe tribes. By age twenty-eight, he was the unchallenged leader of the Borjigin Mongols.

In 1206 Temujin assembled a great council, or *kuriltai*, to choose one ruler over Asia. Mongol chieftains overwhelmingly proclaimed Temujin *khagan*, a khan of khans. They also gave him the glorified title of *genghis*, possibly from the Turkish word for ocean. Temujin became Genghis Khan, "Supreme Ruler over the Ocean" to the Mongols and "Emperor of Emperors" to the Persians. Proud Genghis announced that from that day forward his people would be known as *Koko-Mongols*, "The Heavenly Blue Mongols." The news brought great feasting in Genghis's honor with singers, dancers, jugglers, magicians, food, and drink.

When the celebration ended, Genghis instituted new government and military systems. There were appointments, special duties, and a detailed code of laws prescribing everything from total submission to Mongol lords to methods for killing animals. Genghis organized the camp with his royal silk-hung tent central to the others. He invited representatives of various religions to attend his meetings and offer advice. Among these religious leaders was the lama of Sakya, the religious head of Tibet. This move marked the first spread of Buddhism, or Tibetan Lamaism, into Mongolia. Until then, Mongols practiced Shamanism.

An engraving showing Temujin khagan or Genghis Khan

Genghis also charged a defecting Uighur with responsibility for writing Mongol history. The document, *The Secret History of the Mongols*, detailed Mongol daily life and the career of Genghis Khan. The book was the first written in the new Mongol script, which developed from Uighur.

As the empire spread, Genghis needed ways to send timely messages over long distances. He wanted a spy system in neighboring countries. The answer to his communication problems was the *yam*—a network of riders. Genghis ordered local

An illustration by N. Pranishnikoff shows the Mongol horsemen who were considered unconquerable.

chiefs to keep fresh mounts ready so riders could change horses every twenty minutes. Messengers with bandaged and oiled bodies for protection against brutal weather rode continuously day and night to transmit information anywhere in the empire. A good rider could cover 225 miles (362 kilometers) a day by changing horses frequently.

The real strength of the empire was its extraordinary, disciplined army. Genghis organized men into trained units of tens, hundreds, thousands, and ten thousands that could be called into action quickly. Soldiers wore heavy leather armor called *lamellar* that was invented in China, and they carried strong bows, lances, and swords. Each soldier owned between three and twenty horses, so he could change horses daily. Units carried collapsible bridges for surprise river and moat crossings. With their superior equipment, strength, and strategies, the Mongol army was unconquerable.

To Genghis Khan, war was the ultimate experience. He once

said, "The greatest pleasure is to vanquish your enemies and chase them before you to rob them of their wealth and see those dear to them bathed in tears, to ride their horses." The thrill of war led Genghis and his masterful army into the Russian steppe to the north, as far west as the Middle East and Eastern Europe, south, and through the Great Wall in northern China. He formed the greatest empire consolidated under single leadership in the then-known world.

Mongols employed terror as a means of defeating their enemies. They ruthlessly ravaged opponents, killing and maiming soldiers and civilians, setting entire villages afire, and then driving survivors ahead of the Mongol army toward the next fight. However, once fighting ended, Mongols allowed those who were alive to retain their varying cultures. Local citizens paid taxes as homage to the khan's warlords. And they provided luxuries, such as food, silk, and metals, that the Mongols had grown to appreciate. But religion, art, education, and government were left essentially unchanged. Occasionally Mongols settled with conquered people and became part of their culture, or they brought foreign customs back to the steppe.

Genghis Khan died in August of 1227. Mongolian tradition dictated that the body of a ruler be hidden. Accordingly, Genghis's body was buried somewhere at the top of Mount Burham-Kaldun as he wished. The earth was dug up and trees planted over his plot. Those who buried Genghis Khan were executed so the exact location was unknown within a few years.

One story says that a certain clan was elected to guard the site forever. If travelers searched for the grave, Mongols were silent about its whereabouts. But the legend of the Great Kahn was passed on through the centuries.

Chapter 4

FALL OF THE EMPIRE

Before Genghis Khan's death, he divided the Mongol Empire into four kingdoms, or *khanates*. He directed that a son or grandson administer each portion under the central rule of one son, who was to be elected khan by the kuriltai. At the death of each future khan, all Genghis's descendants were to meet in a kuriltai and choose another khan.

OGODEI

Two years after Genghis's death, an assembly of nobles confirmed Ogodei, his third son, as khagan. Ogodei's reign became one of the most important in the empire's history. Ogodei transformed the empire from a nomadic military organization to a centralized bureaucratic state.

The Mongol khan supervised his large kingdom from Karakorum, a central stronghold near the Orhon Gol that was founded by his father in 1220. Karakorum, once a tent village of nomads, blossomed into the economic, cultural, and political center of the united empire. Markets thrived and skilled laborers flocked to the wealthy city. Artisans built and decorated

Kublai Khan, the last of the great Mongol princes, proclaimed himself emperor of Mongolia and united China in 1279.

columned buildings and created lovely works of clay, metal, and jeweled art. Travelers marveled that twelve different religions, including Buddhism and Christianity, coexisted side by side.

On the military front, Ogodei consolidated his father's conquests over North China, India, Persia, and the Russian steppe. In addition, his armies savagely pressed into Tibet, Siberia, and Bulgaria. Warriors were about to invade Vienna, Austria, when Ogodei died, some say from too much wine. As observed in Genghis Khan's will, all royal princes returned to Karakorum to select a successor. Vienna was spared.

KUBLAI KHAN

Kuyuk, Ogodei's son and successor, planned to continue the conquest of Europe. However, his death after only two years as

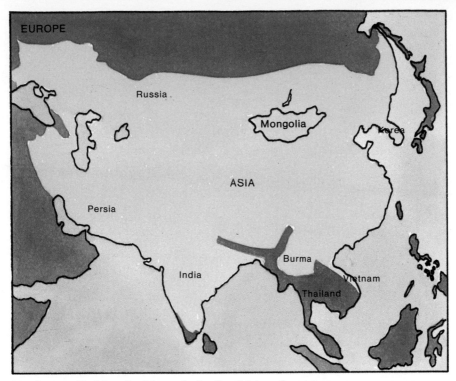

Land controlled by the Mongols in the thirteenth century.
The black outline shows the area of present-day Mongolia.

khan interfered with this goal. Kuyuk's cousin and the next khan, Mangu, brought new military vigor to the empire and renewed interest in conquering all of Asia. His brutal armies under command of his younger brother, Kublai, pressed deep into China. Just as China began to crumble, however, Mangu died.

The Mongol Empire reached its peak during the rule of Kublai Khan. Kublai brought all of China under his command and penetrated into present-day Korea, Burma, Laos, Vietnam, and Cambodia. To govern his vast South Asian conquests, Kublai moved the Mongol capital from Karakorum to Peking in China. In 1279 he proclaimed himself emperor of Mongolia and united China and established the Yuan Dynasty. Kublai was China's first foreign emperor and the only Mongol khan to rule his empire from a permanent kingdom.

After conquering China and Korea, Kublai Khan demanded that

Japan submit also. The proud Japanese ignored his order. In response, the khan's fleet successfully attacked Hakata Bay. That night after battle, a surprise storm forced Mongol ships to leave the bay. Once at sea, storm overtook the fleet and sank 200 ships and 13,500 soldiers. In 1281, Kublai sent a stronger fleet. This time, there were 4,400 ships with 142,000 troops. Japanese rulers prayed to their Shinto gods as the massive fleet prepared to invade. The answer to their prayers was another more devastating storm the Japanese called *kamikaze*, or "divine wind." Kublai Khan's fleet was almost destroyed. After the storm Kublai concentrated on rebuilding the empire already under his domain. And Japan avoided foreign rule for the next six-and-a-half centuries, until World War II.

Until Kublai's reign, the Mongol empire grew rich at the expense of conquered countries. However, China had been the mecca of culture and economy in Asia. Kublai knew that if he drained wealth from this great land there would be widespread rebellion.

Chinese counselors helped Kublai restructure the empire so everyone enjoyed the wealth. The new dynasty established schools following Chinese style and created a Mongolian school of art to rival the Chinese. Administrators rewrote legal codes, reduced taxes, promoted trade, and rebuilt the battered Chinese economy to raise revenue for the Mongol Empire. And Kublai began building a grand capital that became known as the Forbidden City.

News of Kublai's rich court spread to the Western world. Marco Polo, a trusted Venetian visitor and diplomat of Kublai's court, wrote *Description of the World*, a book detailing his seventeen-year stay within the advanced Yuan Dynasty. Polo cited the khan's

Marco Polo (left) was a guest of the Yuan Dynasty for seventeen years. Because movable type had been invented and books (above) could be printed, Polo was able to tell the world about the East in his book, Description of the World.

postal network of horseback riding and the mining of coal or "black stone." He also described inventions Europeans never dreamed of—paper, paper money, printing, and the compass.

MONGOL DECLINE

All the attention on China led to rebellion on the steppe. Moving the capital to Peking helped China recover. But it drew Mongols into China and separated the Mongols of China from their relatives on the steppe. For the next thirty years there was unrest among steppe rulers, infighting that eventually weakened the empire. Gradually, the northern and western khanates of the empire went separate ways.

After Kublai's death in 1294, the empire slowly fell apart as the Mongols were absorbed into Chinese society. Succeeding emperors of China had short and troubled reigns. Soon the

45

Mongol armies weakened. Discontented Chinese seized the opportunity to regain their country. In 1368, a group led by Chu Yuen-chang drove the last of Kublai's nine successors from Peking and Chu declared himself Emperor Hung-wu of the Ming Dynasty. Chu's army chased the battered Mongol armies north across the border and destroyed the Mongol capital of Karakorum. Northern Mongols continued to threaten Chinese borders until the fifteenth century. However, Mongols never played a major role in South Asian and Indian history again.

Mongol hold on western lands became equally fragile. The descendants of Kublai Khan who ruled the west steppe did not enforce the same safeguards against vying factions that Kublai had employed in China. The Mongols of Persia, the Ilkhans, followed steppe traditions in their court. They never adapted to local Islamic culture. After many violent uprisings, western Mongols retreated to the steppe and left administration of their provinces to the Turks.

The Golden Horde, a name given to Mongols ruling the Russian steppe, lasted the longest of Genghis's empires. Their court at Sarai on the Volga River became a thriving trade center. Nomadic Mongols felt comfortable on this steppe and eventually mixed with Turkish tribes there to become Russian Tartars. Intermingling soon weakened Mongol power, however. When Russian princes asserted their independence in the fifteenth century, Mongol chiefs offered little resistance.

BUDDHISM TAKES HOLD

With the disintegration of the Mongol Empire, steppe life reverted to the way life was before Genghis Khan. Independent nomad tribes constantly fought each other and raided lands to the south. Occasionally, a chieftain sought to reunite the Mongols. But no leader ever gained the prominence of Genghis and his descendants.

By the mid-fifteenth century, two main tribes rose on the steppe. The Khalkhas occupied land north of the Gobi. And the Oirats lived in the Altai Mountains of western Mongolia. Their constant quarreling kept the steppe in turmoil for centuries. Only common hatred of the Chinese, who refused to trade with Mongol barbarians, brought them together.

As war resumed with the Chinese, another khan united the Khalkhas and defeated Chinese raiding parties. Altan Khan was a forceful, yet sensible, leader. He wanted to negotiate trade concessions from the Chinese rather than conquer them. Negotiations took almost twenty years. But in 1571 he finalized a treaty, thus ending border disputes that had continued for over two centuries. Altan Khan became the most powerful Mongol prince since the Yuan Dynasty.

Altan's leadership brought renewed wealth for the Mongols. It also signaled large-scale Mongol conversion to Lamaism. Altan agreed to grant a Tibet religious leader the title *dalai lama*, or universal monk. In exchange the lama declared that Altan's ancestors were descended from Kublai Khan, the most famous Mongol Buddhist. Altan believed this connection would give him more political clout.

The lama made his headquarters in the centralized town of Urga, which later became the Mongolian capital Ulan Bator. From this base, he actively sought converts to his form of Buddhism. The next lama returned to Tibet to conduct religious matters for both countries. By then, most of Mongolia was transformed into a highly controlled Buddhist state. Now political authority came from Tibet rather than local Mongol chieftains. Monasticism became a desirable occupation and claimed large numbers of the nation's capable young men. By the mid-1700s, Buddhism accomplished what centuries of warfare were unable to do — weaken the khan's authority and sap Mongolian military strength.

THE MANCHUS

Erosion of Mongol independence began in the seventeenth century. Warfare had progressed beyond nomadic strategies. Mongol armies had difficulty competing against neighbors who fought with guns and cannons. At the same time, Mongolia was being squeezed by two growing powers who were intent upon expansion — Russia and China. Mongol tribes formed and broke alliances with Russians to the northwest and the rising Manchus of northeast China.

In the early 1600s, a Manchu chieftain named Nurhachi rose to power after the fall of the Ming Dynasty. Nurhachi organized his tribe from present-day Manchuria into military divisions under a single flag or banner and proclaimed himself founder of the Ch'ing Dynasty. Then he and his followers moved southward to conquer all of China in the name of the Manchu Empire.

Initially, Manchus included willing Mongol tribes under their banners and treated them as equals. But Nurhachi remembered the potential threat when Mongols banded together. When their rule was secure in China, the Manchus launched a series of actions against Mongols north of the Gobi. By the mid-eighteenth century, the Manchus completely dominated Mongolia.

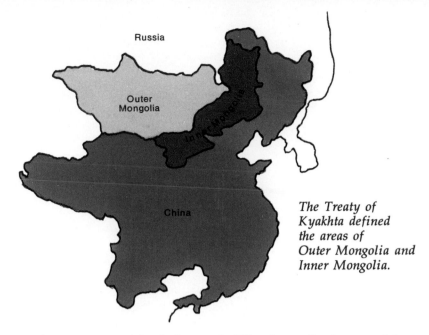

The Treaty of Kyakhta defined the areas of Outer Mongolia and Inner Mongolia.

Meanwhile, Russia pushed through Siberia and advanced into Mongol territories from the north. Dual expansion of Russian and Manchu forces soon led to conflict between these two powers. Russia, already involved in European wars, proposed negotiations with China. In 1689, the enemies settled their disputes with the Treaty of Nerchinsk. The treaty governed Russian-Manchu relations until 1727. The same year, the empires concluded another treaty to set stricter boundaries for Mongolia. The commercial Treaty of Kyakhta renamed the area north of the Gobi Outer Mongolia, which is the country as it stands today. The area east of the Gobi became Inner Mongolia.

SPREAD OF BUDDHISM

At first, Nurhachi modeled Manchu laws and taxes on Mongol systems. He even commanded that Manchu writing be developed from Mongol script. However, as the Manchu conquered more of China, Tibet, Korea, and Mongolia, their military organization was transformed by Chinese religious and administrative institutions. Although Manchus were nomadic herders like Mongols, the empire they built was more Chinese in character.

Manchu rule of Mongolia was a strange combination of neglect and tight control. From the mid-eighteenth to mid-nineteenth centuries, the Manchus mainly ignored Outer Mongolia. Inner Mongolia became part of mainstream China. Throughout Mongolia, however, religious leaders held most of the power. The Manchu installed their "Living Buddha" as supreme religious leader in Mongolia. The Living Buddha was a monk who answered to the Manchu rather than local Mongol chiefs. Since most Mongols were Buddhists, monks became the political and religious voice of Mongolia. The Manchu successfully reduced the influence of most tribal chieftains and made Mongols dependent upon Manchu will.

Buddhism altered almost every aspect of Mongolian life. By the late nineteenth century, a network of 740 monasteries laced the countryside, claiming 40 percent of Outer Mongolian males as monks. Custom dictated that the firstborn male of every family join a monastery. Monks were not allowed to marry or have children. With so many men involved with the church, Mongolian population growth came to a standstill.

Most of Mongolian wealth, education, and enterprise rested with monks, whose chief job was to pray. Monks owned monasteries and much of the livestock. The only other landowners were a small aristocratic class. Monasteries became centers for trade and urbanization. Men who were not monks worked the land as serfs to support monastic life. Mongols got caught in a cycle of continuously working for the church and owing China for necessities. Cut off from the rest of the world, Mongolia ceased to progress.

Chapter 5

A CHANGING LAND

REVOLUTION

Manchu China dominated Outer Mongolia for more than two centuries. During that time, China kept Mongolia isolated from the rest of the world. Some Mongols, like the Khalkha tribes, were able to recognize China and still guard their independence. Others, like the Buryats, migrated to Russian Siberia. For most Mongols, time stood still. They had little knowledge of the industrialization that was looming in the West. Their main concern was freeing their land from foreign occupation.

When the Chinese overthrew the Manchu's decaying Ch'ing Dynasty, Mongolia seized the opportunity to revolt. On November 18, 1911, Mongols claimed loyalty to the Manchu, not the Chinese, and announced their independence. Urga nobles selected the head of the Mongolian Buddhist church, Jebtsun Damba Khutukhtu, as ruler and chased Chinese troops from their land.

Russia encouraged its neighbor's success. Two weeks after the new government formed, Russia signed an agreement with Mongolia that recognized a separate Mongolian state. Then Russia offered assistance in the form of money, arms, ammunition, and personnel to train the young army. Russia wanted trade privileges and a chance to create a secure buffer zone between itself and China. However, Russia never thought of Mongolia as completely independent.

Initially, China had no intention of permitting Mongolia's autonomy. But there were many unsettled problems at home. And Russia's quick response embarrassed the Chinese. Two years after separation, Mongolia's two neighbors signed a pact whereby Russia agreed to China's rule over Inner Mongolia, and China recognized independence for Outer Mongolia. Essentially, Mongolia became a Russian protectorate.

Mongolia relied on Russia for its political existence. However, everyday steppe life still depended upon monks and nobles, who claimed the country's power, education, and wealth. Independence brought little change for the common people.

SHAKY BEGINNINGS

Mongolia's lifeline to independence thinned as Russia turned its attention toward World War I. Soon the Russian Revolution of 1917 toppled tsarist rule and replaced it with a people's Communist government, the Union of Soviet Socialist Republics. Upheaval at home ended Russian assistance to Mongolia. China quickly moved in to reassert control over Mongolia.

Cruel Chinese warlords reigned. The oppressed Mongols sought relief from exiled Russian Baron Roman von Ungern-Sternberg and his White Russian troops. Ungern promised to rid Mongolia of the Chinese. In return, Mongols paid for his services and allowed him to use Urga as his base of operations against Soviet

The statue of Sukhe Bator contains a relief in the base, which shows Mongol partisans (mostly nomads) who fought during the revolution.

Communist forces. Early in 1921, five thousand White Russian troops swarmed into Urga and drove out the Chinese. At first, Mongols were overjoyed. Then the "Mad Baron" terrorized Mongolia searching for Soviet Communists. The baron's murderous White Russians and Chinese reappearance spurred a ground swell of support for Mongolian nationalism.

Two underground resistance leaders, Sukhe Bator and Khorloghiyin Choibalsan, appealed to the infant Soviet government, formerly Russia, for aid in ousting the invaders. In response, Soviets assembled the Revolutionary Provisional Government of Mongolia within its borders. Soviet military joined forces with Sukhe Bator's meager Mongol troops and prepared to retake Mongolia. In the summer of 1921 the Soviet-Mongolian army stormed the occupied capital city, executed Baron Ungern, and established an independent government under the Living

Photographs from the late 1920s show Inner Mongolian residents, a young woman (right) wearing the customary headdress consisting of amber beads and silver ornaments and a young man (far right) carrying all his belongings in a bedroll.

Buddha. Every year since, Mongols celebrate July 11 as the anniversary of the triumphant people's revolution. And Sukhe Bator is hailed as the country's greatest hero for founding the modern Mongolian state.

When the Living Buddha died, the people's government refused to find a replacement, thus ending rule by lama. On November 26, 1924, the new government headed by Premier Choibalsan proclaimed its independent state the Mongolian People's Republic. Urga became the capital city and was renamed Ulan Bator, meaning "Red Hero." Leaders wrote a new constitution based on the Soviet model. In the months that followed, the Soviet-guided government established a bank with national currency, a tax system, and trade agreements with the Soviet Union. Modern Mongolia was born.

THE HARD ROAD TO DEMOCRACY

At independence, Mongols were a nation of largely illiterate nomads, who were unprepared to develop a modern state and society. Loyalties to traditional authorities ran deep. Transition was so slow that the reform government faction directed from Moscow pushed for radical change.

Extremists overthrew conservative elements of the Mongolian People's Revolutionary party. Then they launched programs that were as repressive and intolerant as previous reforms. The program called for government ownership of church and secular property and the organization of workers into collective farms and ranches where everyone had joint ownership under government supervision. Transportation and trade were nationalized. Foreign relations policy excluded trade with any country other than the Soviet Union.

New policies were executed harshly. The government seized control of 837 estates by 1932 and banned private industry. Heads of households, as well as anyone opposed to collectives, were killed or imprisoned. To reduce lingering Buddhist influence, high-level monks were murdered or sent to concentration camps. Ordinary monks were forced into the army or a collective farm.

Change was too quick and violent, even for the one-time warriors. Sporadic rebellion erupted throughout Outer Mongolia. The government's response was to clamp down harder. The power of the monks and nobles ended along with private trade. However, the inexperienced government had no effective state-run replacement. The herding society was too slow to adopt new ways. Food shortages developed as the country was on the brink of civil war.

The Mongolian People's Revolutionary party, backed by the Soviet Union, shifted direction and stopped forcing people onto collective farms. Instead, they began the long, slow process of persuading citizens to join collective farms and craft *artels*, or

The Japanese army would have found this main highway in Inner Mongolia difficult to maneuver if they had tried to send an army against the Soviets during World War II.

associations, through reeducation and propaganda. Gradually, communism began to replace Buddhism, and collective industry displaced much of the nomadism. But the basic transformation from an agrarian country into an industrial-agrarian country is still being tackled.

FOREIGN RELATIONS

The Soviet Union continued to have a major impact upon the Mongolian government. Choibalsan listened to Soviet direction and provided Moscow with livestock and raw materials. In 1939, Soviet troops helped Mongols fight back invading Japanese and generally kept China from crossing Mongolia's southern border, a boundary China never really accepted. When the Soviets declared war on Japan during World War II, Mongolia followed. Once again, the Soviets crushed intruding Japanese troops.

The architectural influence of the Soviet Union can be seen in this building (left) and train station (above) in Ulan Bator.

After the war, China agreed to grant Outer Mongolia independent status. However, China required that the people of Mongolia prove their desire for independence by open vote. The entire Mongol adult population voted 100 percent for autonomy from China. On January 5, 1946, China finally recognized a separate Mongolia and agreed to exchange foreign diplomats. With Mongolia at peace with China and Japan, the Socialist nation directed its energy toward modernization and building a national industry.

The pace of change quickened after 1962. Mongolia had been a member of the United Nations for one year and had just joined the Communist bloc's Council for Mutual Economic Assistance. Now other Communist countries invested in Mongolian industry. They built factories and sent technicians to train Mongolian workers. China, too, sent workers when relations with the Soviet Union were friendly.

Still the Soviet Union had the greatest presence in Mongolia. The country's international mail, telephone, and cables to the outside world went through the Soviet Union. By the mid-1980s, there were an estimated sixty thousand Soviet troops stationed within Mongolian borders. Soviet-Chinese relations thawed and cooled, depending upon the number of Soviet troops lining China's border. Besides military, there were many Soviet technicians helping Mongols develop their minerals. In the town of Erdenet alone, about ten thousand workers out of thirty-seven thousand residents were Soviets.

Toward the end of the decade, the Soviet Union entered a period of nonintervention and peaceful foreign relations. Soviet leaders met with representatives from China and the United States to reduce tensions between the world powers. To appease the Chinese, the Soviets announced plans to withdraw 75 percent of the Soviet troops stationed in Mongolia.

At the same time, Mongolia disclosed efforts to revive its independent heritage while seeking a role in world politics. Genghis Khan, once scorned as a warrior, became honored as founder of Mongolia. Officials named a new drink and hotel in Ulan Bator after him and rock singers sang his praises. New signs appeared in the old script to replace the Russian Cyrillic alphabet. Defense spending was reduced by 11 percent to free money for advancing the industrial Socialist state. Additionally, people took to the streets to protest single-party rule. A group called the Mongolian Democratic party spearheaded a movement for free elections, an end to the single-party system, freedom of religion, free press, and trade with whichever country offers the best terms. In the spring of 1990, these dreams became reality. After many peaceful protests, the ruling Mongolian People's Revolutionary

Above left: Before the election in 1990, a voter asks a question of a candidate running in his district. Left: Dressed in traditional clothing, voters wait to cast their ballots. Above: Campaign workers from the Social Democratic party hang posters, containing a picture of Genghis Khan, before the July 28 election.

party stepped down as the only power in Mongolian society, ending almost seven decades of rule. Although the Communist party retained control, free elections led to a multiparty system of government and other freedoms under democracy.

This spirit of openness also led Mongolia to establish diplomatic relations with the United States. More than seventeen countries already had embassies in Ulan Bator, including several from the non-Communist countries of India, France, Japan, and Britain. Mongols opened diplomatic relations with more than fifty-two countries. For the first time, Mongolia sent representatives to other countries. The world was discovering the wonderful secrets of this once-great nation.

Above: Mongols listen to speeches at a political rally in March 1990.
Below: A campaign worker answers the telephone at the Mongolian National Progressive party headquarters. Campaign posters are behind her.

Chapter 6

A LEAP ACROSS TIME

Before the revolution, Mongolia's economy was one of the most backward in Asia. Mongols had to build their new country from the beginning. Traditional practices guided the people. Lamas supposedly claimed that worldly education, especially for women, was sinful. There was a lack of industry and almost total illiteracy. There were few people scattered throughout the land. Most were without money and technical or scientific skills to invest in Mongolia's dream of industrialization. That is why it was so incredible that Mongols transformed their backward feudal economy into a developing Socialist state in less than seventy-five years. Worker-controlled production of goods replaced oppressive conditions under nobles and monks. Mongolia inched slowly on its way toward modernization.

GOVERNMENT REORGANIZATION

The chief vehicle for change was government reorganization. State powers were transferred to the people, who provided the machinery to make reforms work. With new government came sweeping changes in social, political, and economic areas.

Today, workers choose local and national government officials from members of the Mongolian People's Revolutionary party

(MPRP), the main political party, and a handful of opposition parties that have organized since the move toward democracy began. The 1940 constitution dictates that primary power to enact laws rests with the People's Great Khural, or National Assembly. However, country leadership stems from the ten-member Politburo or Central Committee. Khural representatives are elected for three-year terms by popular vote. One representative serves every twenty-five hundred people. Representatives meet three days of each year to establish central laws for the country.

Between annual meetings, a seven-member Presidium of the People's Great Khural administers the government. The Presidium handles day-to-day affairs by appointing a Council of Ministers. The Presidium chairperson functions as head of state, mainly in name only. Actual control rests with the premier who heads the Council of Ministers and leads the party.

The Mongolian People's Republic administers justice through a court system and office of the Procurator. The People's Great Khural votes for Supreme Court justices and appoints the Procurator. In turn, lower administrative units elect their own courts and appoint lower-level procurators. The Supreme Court and Procurator answer to the People's Great Khural and Presidium.

Local government is broken into progressively smaller administrative units, each managed by a smaller Khural. Mongolia has eighteen *aimaks*, or provinces, plus the capital of Ulan Bator. Aimak residents elect deputies to the Khural. These deputies elect judges for local courts.

Somons, or counties, and independent areas compose the next lower administrative level. Leaders of these units frequently hold powerful positions within livestock, trade, and agricultural

An elderly woman about to vote asks for help in reading and marking her ballot.

cooperatives as well. Still, the greatest influence within each aimak and somon is the local party organization. In the past the MPRP ran the People's Great Khural, cooperatives, and executive committees on every level. More recently, opposition parties seized authority in some areas.

Party involvement is critical to carrying out government policy. Therefore, the MPRP created a Revolutionary Youth League to get citizens involved early. The Revolutionary Youth League is particularly important because half the Mongolian population is under age twenty-five. In 1987 the MPRP had 88,150 members, while the Revolutionary Youth League boasted more than 200,000 young people. Introduction to party ideology for these youngsters begins in Young Pioneers' summer camp and clubs.

Another political organization in larger towns and provinces is the Federation of Mongolian Women. This group has over five thousand women's councils specifically responsible for monitoring equality for all women over sixteen years of age. Before the revolution, women had few rights in Mongolia. Afterward, Mongolia became one of the first Asian countries to legislate that women receive full political and economic equality. With the mid-1980 elections, 25 percent of the People's Great Khural deputies were women and 29 percent of local Khural deputies were women. Additionally, the government enacted a host of laws to support women's dual roles of bearing and raising children and employment in the national economy.

EDUCATE FOR THE ECONOMY

Revolution brought drastic changes in education. The Mongolian People's Republic saw education as a way to build the young nation. Required education would be effective for converting citizens to Communist ideology. Education offered the surest path to transforming Mongolia's nomadic society into a semi-industrialized economy.

Mongols borrowed much from the Soviet Union's system of education. Textbooks were Russian translations and teachers were on loan from the Soviet Union. With strong Soviet support, Mongols made education a top priority. By the mid-1980s, more than 80 percent of the population could read and write. That figure exceeded numbers from many industrial nations. From a country without public schools, Mongols developed an educational system of general elementary and secondary schools, a network of preschools, special schools for students with handicaps, thirty-seven vocational and technical training schools, and five institutions of higher learning.

Currently the Ministry of People's Education requires every child over eight to attend free school for eight years. At eight years of age, children are considered old enough to stay at boarding school or to ride on horseback to school across the

Primary (left) and intermediate (right) schoolchildren

steppe. In sparsely populated areas, seven of ten children attend boarding school. A child may leave for school in September and not return until May, except for holidays. Some children extend their time away by going to summer camp.

Mongolian elementary education emphasizes practical subjects. Education begins in kindergarten along with reading and writing. Above all, law dictates that students learn the discipline that is required for being good citizens. Instructors teach children strict respect for elders and teachers.

Students who want more than eight years of education must pass rigorous exams. Promising students are tracked for technical and scientific studies either at home or abroad. High test scores may mean that the state pays all higher education bills. Young Mongols view higher education as the main avenue to success. Some ten thousand students seek higher education. Half of them are women. Students at institutions of higher learning can study

A high school chemistry class (left) and Mongolian State University (right)

engineering, mathematics, biology, chemistry, economics, social science—every field of academic learning that could contribute to building the economy.

ECONOMIC GROWTH

The People's Revolutionary party introduced economic development plans in slow, steady stages, each spanning five years. Initial plans stressed increasing stock breeding to raise money for investment in modern industry. Animals provided unlimited sources of raw products the Mongols already knew how to handle. Gradually, Mongols, with the aid of their Communist neighbors, introduced light manufacturing of animal products such as foods, leather, and wool. In the past twenty years, more emphasis was on expanding manufacturing and developing technology to explore and utilize Mongolia's rich mineral resources.

A young herder with his grazing horses (left); camels in the Gobi Desert (right)

HERDING AND FARMING

Even with rapid change, livestock remains the mainstay of Mongolia's economy. By the mid-1980s the nation claimed more than twenty-four million animals in its huge pasture. More than half of these were sheep. The rest were goats, horses, cattle, and camels.

Most livestock are owned collectively by workers on cooperative farms. If a herder sells or butchers any animals, all herders in the cooperative share the profits. However, the state directs how and when wandering herders move and raise their flocks.

The government goes to great lengths to settle nomads. Families of herders who leave pastoral life receive housing in permanent settlements complete with schools, health care, shops, and television. Farming allows herders to breed rare animals only seen in nearby China. For example, most workers of the early Mongolian People's Republic had never seen pigs or chickens.

A tractor pulls a trailerload of agricultural workers

Their children knew the tale of a hungry wolf who huffed and puffed until he blew down the ger of four little goats. American children know this story as *The Three Little Pigs*. Today there are pig and chicken farms in central and northern Mongolia.

Agriculture has made great strides recently. Most early farms were in Inner Mongolia in the hands of the Chinese. With Soviet-supplied farm equipment, irrigation systems, and technology, huge tracts of Outer Mongolian land have been plowed for grains, hay, fruits, and vegetables. Visitors to the semidry Gobi see wells and irrigation canals in areas once reserved for nomads, camels, and deer. Throughout Mongolia there are more than three hundred cattle breeding and agricultural farms.

HUNTING AND FISHING

Rich wildlife resources have been a staple of Mongolian economy for centuries. Proof of this wealth can be seen in cliff drawings and folk paintings that go back thousands of years.

Fishermen (left) and a colorfully attired hunter (right)

Today the government controls commercial fishing and hunting. However, fish are rarely eaten by Mongols. Clear, swift northern waterways offer an abundance of large salmon, trout, and whitefish for export. Frigid winter temperatures provide natural freezing for easy transport to fisheries.

Pelts from furbearing animals bring considerable foreign revenue into Mongolia. The government has set tight controls on hunting to ensure that supplies continue. Commercial hunters belong to the Huntsmen's Association of the Mongolian People's Republic and must pay for a hunting license. In the mid-1980s, there were about thirty thousand association members. Annually they killed between two and three million animals, especially the prized marmot.

Large tracts of land within each mountain range have been set aside as national wildlife reservations. The government banned hunting of fish and rare animals such as the Mongolian horse, wild camel, antelope, and deer. In addition, the state opened breeding farms for mink, foxes, and sable.

INDUSTRY AND MINING

The success of modern Mongolia lies in its ability to diversify industry for export while still providing basic food, clothing, and shelter for its people. Initial industrialization developed from boundless supplies of animal products. Mongols built leather tanneries and shoe factories, processing plants for wool, knitted garment mills, dairies, and meat-processing plants. The government reinvested profits from these ventures to build additional plants.

In the 1960s Mongols realized that to develop major industrial centers they needed basic brickworks, power stations, and cement plants. Construction became a blossoming national industry. This and other industries were established with foreign investment and workers. Countries in the Communist bloc's Council for Mutual Economic Assistance built factories, trained Mongolian workers, and imported finished products. Often, the investing country named factories after one of their political heroes. For example, the Wilhelm Pieck Carpet Factory is named after an East German politician. When China and the Soviet Union got along, China offered money and battalions of workers in blue uniforms that Mongols called "blue bees." Thousands of Chinese settled in Ulan Bator to build a department store, sports stadium, hospital, hotel, and housing. Others built power stations, roads, and bridges. Many have since left the country as Chinese-Mongolian relations worsened.

Major industrial centers sprouted in Darkhan, Choybalsan, and Erdenet with numerous projects dotting the countryside for Mongolia's most promising industry—mining. Once Mongolia was thought to be only a poor nation of herders. But recent

A power station (left) and a textile mill

geological surveys discovered vast deposits of coal, iron, tin, copper, gold, silver, tungsten, petroleum, and rare metals used in steel and tungsten production, such as fluorspar and molybdenum. The Gobi has become a newer source of oil, salt, and shale.

Mongolian trading partners were mainly Council for Mutual Economic Assistance countries. The Soviet Union particularly remained Mongolia's principal source of credit. Exports and imports were transported through the Soviet Union by air or railroad. However Mongolia sought more ties with the West as the Soviet economy worsened. In 1991 United States President George Bush granted Mongolia most-favored-nation trade status. This title accompanied lower tariffs on Mongolian goods and more joint business ventures between the United States and Mongolia, especially in dairy products, wool processing, and oil exploration. Animals and their by-products of meat, butter, wool,

Although the runway at the airport is flat, it still provides a bumpy landing.

hair, hides, and fur account for almost 90 percent of Mongolian exports. Other principal export products are cement and lumber. Major imports are machinery, fuel, metals, chemicals, fertilizers, and raw materials for food production.

Mongols transact these trades with currency called *tughrik*. Money flows through Mongolbank or the Mongolian State Trade Office.

TRANSPORTATION

Horses and two-humped camels provided excellent steppe transportation for centuries. But as industry, cities, and the seeds of tourism developed, there was greater need to establish broader transportation links.

Nowadays travelers and goods arrive in Mongolia either by air or railroad from China or the Soviet Union. The Trans-Mongolian Railway links Moscow, Ulan Bator, and Beijing. National air

The most economical means of transport are motorcycles in the cities and two-humped camels on the steppe.

service permits travel between Ulan Bator and other countries and between Mongolian provincial capitals. There are no cement runways as in the west. The hard steppe provides a bumpy but flat surface for landing.

Although old ways persist in parts of Mongolia, it is cheaper and easier to ride motorbikes than horses in cities. Similarly, trucks, buses, jeeps, and cars replace most caravans for cross-country travel. Road travel is bumpier than in many countries, however. There are some paved highways, but most travel is over dry, flat steppe earth.

COMMUNICATION

On November 10, 1920, the Mongolian revolutionary press changed the course of history with its first issue of the newspaper *Mongolyn Unen*, meaning "Mongolian Truth." The paper exposed Baron Ungern's monstrous White Russian army and called for a

People's Revolution against all occupying forces. Since that time, the MPR State Committee for Information, Radio, and Television has used newspapers, radio, television, and magazines as powerful tools to reflect state thinking.

Today, *Unen*, a modern version of Mongolia's historic paper, is the leading daily newspaper. Another version, *Zaluchudyn Unen* ("Truth of the Youth"), is published for the Revolutionary Youth League. Each province has its own paper, and there are a growing number of newspapers and magazines publicizing individual and government accomplishments. Together there are more than seventy newspapers and periodicals printed in Mongolia. Periodicals are distributed to almost one hundred countries in Mongol, Russian, English, French, Chinese, and Kazakh languages.

Radio and television are available throughout Mongolia. Radio has the most widespread distribution and plays the greatest role in guiding herders and their thinking. There are estimates that almost every herding family has at least one radio. Television reaches about 60 percent of the population. Two television stations, one local and one from East Europe via satellite, broadcast heavy doses of political programming designed to boost worker productivity. Sprinkled in between are shows about sports, music, dance, theater, and a few Mongolian-made movies.

For centuries, Mongolian history described a country isolated from most of the world. As nations around them advanced, Mongols remained a backward people. But the past seventy-five years have brought a great awakening in Mongolia. Products that once took an entire year to produce in the 1920s are manufactured in one month today. With industrial growth, travel opportunities, and greater communication links with other nations, Mongols are advancing into the twenty-first century.

Chapter 7

THE FABRIC
OF MONGOLIA

In every nation, people have a distinct character. They share a common language, customs, and dress. They eat certain foods and play particular games. Their collective personality in these areas develops with their history. So it is with Mongols. Throughout history, they have been noted for special qualities. Two most striking features are the pride and strength that have carried Mongols through rough times. Mongols are proud of their government, families, and heritage. And their strength makes them hopeful for a bright and peaceful future.

A HEALTHY, GROWING POPULATION

Until the revolution, Mongolia's population remained unusually small. The practice of Lamaism and lack of medical care contributed to low birth rates and early death. Since the revolution there has been emphasis on strengthening population numbers to carry out modernization plans. Today the country boasts a 3 percent annual growth rate, one of the highest in the world. Still, there are only three citizens per square mile (one per square kilometer). Livestock outnumber people thirteen to one.

This family includes the grandmother, the mother and father, and three children.

To encourage larger families, the government offers liberal benefits for births. Families receive payments that increase with each child. Working mothers get forty-five-day maternity leaves. Additionally, a central commission ensures that young children get top priority for government spending in terms of day care and education. Adults volunteer to work an extra Sunday each year for International Children's Day. Their earnings are donated to the central commission's children's fund to promote quality children's programs. A motto for the day is, "Everything for the good of children." Emphasis on having children has changed the population. Half of the Mongols are currently under age eighteen. Sometimes the nation is called "the land of the young."

Health care needed drastic reform if youngsters were to grow old enough to contribute to the economy. In the early 1900s, a Russian study found that 50 percent of Mongolian babies died before they were three years old. Medicine consisted of prayers to

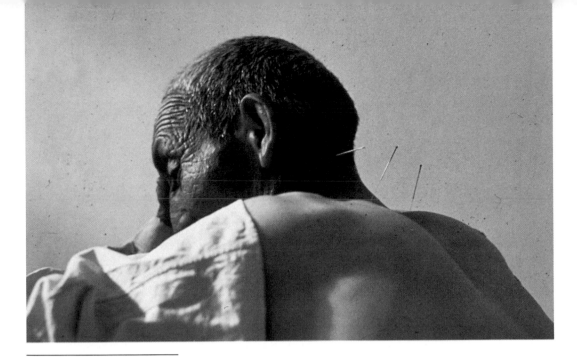

An acupuncture patient

rid the body of evil spirits. Lamaist monks added folk remedies
and different prayers. At the time of the revolution, the country
was without a single trained medical doctor and basic sanitation
was nonexistent.

Today, a network of free health care services safeguards health.
Hospitals or first-aid stations are in every cooperative, somon, and
aimak. Helicopters, which can land on the flat steppe, carry
doctors and nurses to patients in more remote areas. Mongolian
medicine has become a mixture of Western technology, Oriental
practice, and folk treatments. Doctors apply ancient acupuncture
to relieve pain. The therapy involves inserting fine needles into
the skin at key points of the body. Some scholars believe that
acupuncture and the use of herbs came from Tibetan monks. For
flu, muscle, and joint problems, physicians often prescribe hot
mineral baths in volcanic springs of the western Gobi or near
ancient Karakorum. As far back as Genghis Khan, Mongols
recognized the healing properties of special *arshan*, or "water from
a sacred source."

PEOPLE OF MONGOLIA

Of Mongolia's almost two million people, about 90 percent are Mongol. Mongols have well-defined physical features. Their heads are round and they have high cheekbones and flat noses. Their eyes appear slanted because of an extra skin fold covering the eyelid's inner edge. Their hair is dark and coarse on the head and light and thin on the body. Skin color ranges from pale white to yellow brown. Most Mongols have a stocky build.

Khalkhas in the east account for the largest (75 percent) Mongol group. Smaller tribes make up the rest of the Mongol population. These include Oirats in the west and scattered Buryat groups that emigrated from the Soviet Union to the north. Each tribe has its own way of life. Kazakhs and Tuvinians breed stock, while Khotons farm and Tungus hunt. Other non-Mongols in the country are Russian or Chinese, although eastern Europeans work in factories their governments subsidize.

SPEAKING AND WRITING

Each tribe speaks its own form of Mongol dialect. Nevertheless, constant movement over the years made Mongols skillful at conversing with each other. A desire for nationalism after independence encouraged Mongols to consider a standard language. Khalkha was already spoken for official business in Ulan Bator. So Khalkha Mongol became the preferred spoken language in schools and for business. Today, Khalkha is the official steppe language.

The original written Mongol language dated back to thirteenth-century Turkish Uighurs. Script was written vertically from left to

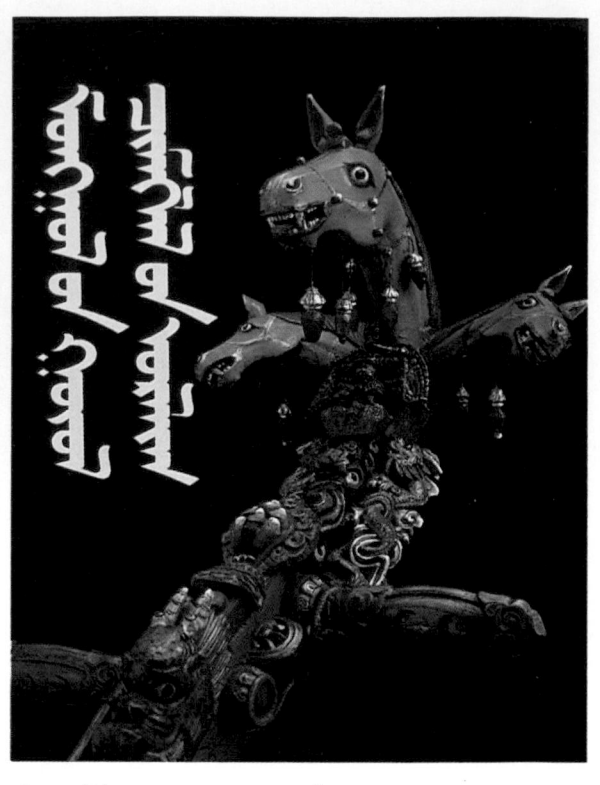

A road sign (left) shows cities in the Russian language. The Mongolian language is used on the book cover (right) of Mongolian Arts and Crafts.

right, similar to Chinese. At the time, ancient writing represented spoken language. But language changed over the centuries. By the twentieth century, early script did not reflect current Mongolian pronunciation. Uneducated Mongols found the writing very hard to learn. With Soviet prodding, the government introduced a revised form of the Russian Cyrillic alphabet in 1946. Two symbols were added to represent Mongolian sounds that were not part of the Russian language. All books and periodicals then were written in the Cyrillic alphabet. And a standard written language was taught throughout the Mongolian People's Republic. Russian was the most widely read and spoken foreign language. However, some Mongols became fluent in German, English, and Chinese. More recently there has been movement toward returning to traditional Mongolian written language.

Mongols have always had great affection for their original language and the way ideas were communicated. Ancient poetic proverbs frequently brighten everyday conversations. For example, Mongols say, "The more difficult one's youth, the easier one's old age," or "With friends you are as broad as the steppe. Without them you are as narrow as the palm of your hand."

HOMES AND CLOTHING

Mongolian clothing and housing has always reflected steppe life-styles. Homes needed to be moved frequently and both dwellings and clothes had to be warm enough to withstand the cold, dry steppe climate. The push to modernize resulted in more Soviet styles in these areas. However, most changes are in cities. Elsewhere, change has come slowly.

On the plains, the most practical dress for weather and riding horses is the traditional *del*. The del is a loose ankle-length robe with a high collar buttoned from left to right. Both men and women wear dels, usually with sheepskin or fox linings to protect against frigid temperatures. Underneath the robe, thick pants and knee-high leather or felt boots are worn. Inside the boots are felt or many-layered cloth socks. Originally, only men wore sashes, called *bous*, at the waist. Today, both sexes tie dels with bright-colored sashes. Men often decorate the sashes with carefully carved tools and ornaments, such as knives, chopsticks, and pouches. Men and women trim their costumes with fine stitchery like silk brocade.

In the 1930s and 1940s, the government moved to simplify dress. Adorned headdresses of married women, felt-rimmed hats, and fancy sashes and cuffs were chief targets for elimination. City life helped to reinforce cosmopolitan dress with more factory-made clothes in stores. In Ulan Bator, workers now wear Western

Mongols wear traditional and modern clothing.

leather shoes and boots. European shirts under dark-colored suits
with ties and overcoats have replaced jeweled hairstyles and
colorful robes. Children at boarding school dress in Western-style
uniforms. Girls wear solid-color dresses, often covered with
aprons, and boys wear corduroy coats and pants. However, at
home, clothes are more colorful and definitely warmer for
herding. The mix of dress serves as a reminder of Mongolia's past
and future.

Stark contrast continues in Mongolian homes. Many Mongols,
particularly outside the city, prefer the traditional homes of their
ancestors called gers (*yurts* in Turkish). Although they are
portable, gers are strong enough to withstand high winds and
several feet of blowing snow. Over the years, ger design has

The frame of this ger is ready to be covered.

remained much the same. The size is still small and light enough to be moved by four camels or two jeeps. Heavy felt made from sheep's wool covers a circular wooden frame. Some families have factory-made gers of aluminum framework. Ropes made of gi-gi-tsao grass secure the felt over the frame. A domelike hole covered by a flap allows smoke to escape and serves as a skylight to the heavens.

Tradition dictates that gers face the southeast. Winds blow from the southeast and the sacred sun rises in the east. Much of the furniture placement also is guided by tradition. A marriage bed goes opposite the entrance. It is never used for sleeping, however. Instead, it holds cushions for sitting and quilts and clothing. In front of the bed is a guest's place of honor facing the entrance.

Stark apartment blocks in Ulan Bator

Guests sit on short wooden stools. Nearby is a chest with a Buddha altar and family pictures. To the east are decorated storage chests and food and kitchen supplies. Stools and chests are often painted orange, a color that means good luck to Mongols. On the west side of the ger are the father's possessions, including saddles and hunting gear. Depending upon a family's wealth, rugs or brightly colored cloths cover the felt walls. Radio, television, permanent flooring, modern stoves, sewing machines, and electricity are some of the few concessions to modernization.

Gers are the main living quarters for herders and farmers on state cooperative farms. In cities, the government has had more success moving people into high-rise Soviet-style apartment buildings. But city people have a strong attachment to their nomadic traditions. Apartments have the same style furnishings as gers. There are brass beds, brightly colored chests, embroidered pillows, Buddha altars, and pictures.

During summers, many city Mongols move into country gers. Others who resist apartments totally live in permanent gers on the edge of the city. Fences add to the sense of private space as rows of gers or rustic cabins line suburban areas around cities like Hatgal or Ulan Bator.

ARTS AND ARTISTS

Until recent moves toward democracy, Mongolian art has mainly celebrated government causes. During the years between revolution and free elections, literature, movies, theater, and other arts were tools of the state. The party expected artists to keep any history, social problems, or feelings about their homeland in line with Socialist thinking. Artists who did not conform were suppressed. Some loosening of controls began in the early 1990s. However, most artists are still accountable to the state for popular support.

Favorite themes in poems, plays, and films ennoble the revolution and the struggles and hopes of the Mongol people to build a new nation. A popular modern play, *Why Me*, tells of a factory manager who is fired for failing to assign responsibility to younger, more creative workers. One of the best-known poets and translators of Russian prose and poetry into Mongol was D. Natsaghdorj. He was a youth during the revolution and played an important role in creating the Young Pioneers. Natsaghdorj's poem "My Homeland" became so popular it was set to music.

Recent attempts to reclaim past history spurred Mongols to revive their rich cultural heritage. Tibetan Buddhism and Chinese influences sparked most early art. However, Mongolian folklore dates back to ancient times. The first folktales were handed down by word of mouth. They frequently were a combination of history, legend, and heroic feats. Old people still amaze youngsters in gers with tales about deeds of great courage. Almost all early Mongolian literature depicts nomadic and hunting scenes, often in poetic forms with rhymes at the beginning or end of lines.

These instructions from Genghis Khan to his army chiefs were recorded in the *Altan tobchi* or "golden chronicle," the seventeenth-century text that is the second-most-famous Mongolian record after the *Secret History*.

> When in contact with others you must be more gentle
> than a small calf, but on a campaign more ferocious
> than a terrible eagle.
> When in the company of friends be more gentle than
> a black calf, but when joined in battle be as merciless
> as the black falcon.

Later writing subjects came from Chinese works. Shamans often adapted Chinese stories into poems and songs as part of Mongolia's oral literature. As Lamaism took hold, more literature had Buddhist themes. Religious plays, called *tsam*, were written by monks and acted by local workers. Older Mongols frequently taught manners to children through religious tales from *Uliger-un dalai*, or "The Sea of Parables." These stories were of animals who learned their lesson after getting into some mischief, similar to Aesop's fables.

Most ancient art was destroyed with the city of Karakorum. Only giant stone tortoises survived. However, detailed and

The door of this simple, white ger is covered with a bright design (left) and a pair of boots (above) is decorated with an intricate design made of appliqué and beads.

colorful designs of early crafts remained in the needlework, leather tooling, sculpting, wickerwork, and metalwork on clothes and household objects. Tibetan Buddhism had great influence on visual arts, too. Monks built grand pagoda temples. They adorned the houses of worship with flags, statues, paintings, felt rugs, and brass decorations.

By the mid-twentieth century, these ornaments gave way to simpler designs. Soviet architects worked with Mongols to construct modern office buildings and apartments. Sculptures created realistic monuments to contemporary heroes—a milkmaid or factory worker. Nyamyn Jamba, a famous sculptor, carved two busts of the revolutionary hero, Sukhe Bator. In art galleries, paintings showed scenes of the countryside and heroic portraits. Art revealed the same realistic views of Socialism as government followed.

Of all the arts, music played the greatest role in Mongolian life. Singing has been a way to relieve loneliness on the steppe. In the 1920s and 1930s, the government tried to discredit traditional music. Still, old songs and instruments survived around campfires and at celebrations. There is a popular legend among Mongols that they invented music for the rest of the world.

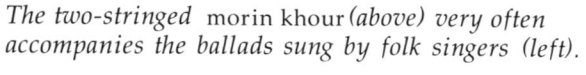

The two-stringed morin khour *(above) very often accompanies the ballads sung by folk singers (left).*

Tender folk songs tell about nature, popular heroes, and romance. Two types of ballads are written in a moody five-tone Oriental scale. "Long songs" tell the sadder story of life on the wide lonely plain. These ballads got their name from the way singers prolong each vowel to make a sorrowful sound. The "short song," which may be longer in length, is cheerier and often funny.

Mongols hear these songs at the Mongolian National Orchestra or at neighborhood sings. Many are played on the hand-carved *morin khour*. This two-stringed instrument was said to be the creation of a man whose beloved horse died. The man used his horse's mane and tail to help form an instrument that looks somewhat like a cross between a viola and cello. A horsehair bow moves against the two strings to make a mournful, sweet sound. The top of the morin khour usually has a horse head for decoration, which helps give the instrument its name of "horse

The Mongolian National Orchestra (left) plays both Asian and European classical music. At discos (right), the latest dance steps are seen.

harmony.'' Herders frequently play the instrument for camels who refuse to nurse their babies. Mongols insist that the music makes ''camels weep and lets their milk flow.''

Another method for making unusual tones is by *hoomi*. Mongol men make hoomi fluttering sounds with their mouth by controlling muscles used in speech. Listeners are sure they hear several notes at once. The sounds are beautiful and strange at the same time. Mongols explain that hoomi came from herders' desire to imitate sounds of nature.

Mongols love many forms of music. The Mongolian National Orchestra performs Asian and European classical music. Jazz blares from Voice of America radio broadcasts. And the Bayan Mongol band and smaller rock groups offer an array of current rock tunes on Western instruments. Many modern songs reflect strong Russian influence.

Dance draws heavily on folk traditions, also. The *Secret History* describes a celebration on the sixteenth day of the fourth lunar month when people gathered to dance. Folk and social dancing is with men and women together, individual dancers, or small groups accompanied by instruments. Mongols usually perform

Above: A contortionist is called a "rubber acrobat." Left: A folk dancer in an elegant costume

folk dances in gaily colored, traditional costumes. More formal ballet and opera performances depict the lives of nomadic characters.

One of the more pleasant results of the Mongolian-Soviet partnership is the circus. Russians open circus performances with offerings of bread and salt as welcome. But the rest of the show is pure Mongolian. The circus takes place in a large ger. Mongols offer their own form of welcome by waving blue scarves. Performing goats, yaks, and wolves replace Russian dancing bears. And circus performers called "rubber acrobats" contort their bodies in bizarre positions rarely seen in the West. Mongolian aerialists sometimes wear costumes of astronauts. They and their clapping audiences are reaching toward the blue skies through the opening of the circus ger.

CELEBRATIONS AND RECREATION

National and family celebrations changed greatly following the revolution. Before independence, religious leaders prescribed special events. However, government attempts to stifle religion effectively eliminated most religious holidays in favor of days supporting state objectives. Now official holidays of the Mongolian People's Republic include International Women's Day on March 8, International Solidarity Day of Working People on May 1 and 2, Anniversary of the Mongolian People's Revolution (National Day) on July 11 and 12, and Anniversary of October Socialist Revolution on November 7 and 8. Only the rituals of New Year's Day and *Nadam* continue from earlier days. Even so, herders celebrate New Year's in February or March, beginning the traditional Mongolian calendar year, and city people celebrate on January 1.

The Nadam festival, or "The Three Games of Men," is the most popular national sporting event. It involves wrestling, archery, and horse races that have been part of Mongolian culture for thousands of years. Since 1921, traditional Nadam competitions begin on July 11 to commemorate Mongolia's independence. Much fanfare in the forms of songs, parades, and dance surrounds each sporting event. Winners receive many awards. In horseback riding, the horse and breeder receive the most honors. Jockeys are usually boys between six and twelve years old, and their job is merely to direct the well-bred horse. In addition to prizes, winning wrestlers earn titles such as "falcon" or "lion," depending upon how many rounds they last with an opponent. Any wrestler winning two or more bouts at a national Nadam receives the title "giant." Mongols find competitions so inspiring

*Youthful jockeys (left) compete in a race. Mongolian wrestlers (right)
wear distinctive outfits of boots, shorts, and a frontless jacket.*

they create poems and songs for winners and tell tales of their
courage long after the festivities end.

Mongolian children have many of the same interests in sports
and games as other children. Youngsters begin learning
techniques of wrestling and horse riding at the age of eight or
nine. They sharpen their sport's skills by entering local Nadam
competitions and watching broadcasts of wrestling contests on
television. Young Mongols also enjoy skiing, volleyball, and more
recently, soccer and basketball. A favorite winter pastime is to
kick a "puck" made of the anklebone of a camel or ox around the
ice. Where it stops determines the number of points a player
receives. Genghis Khan played a version of this game as a child.

When it is too cold to be outside, both young and old enjoy
playing chess or checkers. Families pride themselves on their
beautifully carved chess sets. Carving is a popular recreation for
adults. Mongolian carvers design chess sets with khans for kings,

dogs for queens, and camels for bishops. Women and girls spend some wintry nights embroidering. They make finely decorated pouches and stocking tips for family members to wear. On other nights the entire family sings songs to the morin khour or flips game pieces made from antelope bone, much like marbles in the West.

Certainly traditional family events remain a significant part of Mongolian culture. New babies are formally named at a washing ceremony three days after birth. Mothers or grandmothers bathe the baby in meat broth. Afterward, a monk prays over the baby and gives the child a dunking in holy water. Relatives bring food and gifts to the mother and infant.

When children reach age three years, relatives gather again to take part in a ceremony for the first haircutting. The eldest relation cuts the first lock of hair and offers the child good wishes in words and with a gift. Then everyone else takes a turn. The child's mother gathers the clippings into a silk scarf. Later, she sews the locks into the child's pillow.

Birthdays have been special occasions for children since the time of Genghis Khan. Genghis told his sons that birth was the most important thing a parent could give a child. This sentiment encourages deep respect for parents and ancestors to this day.

Traditional marriages and weddings go through great rituals that include negotiations, poems, songs, many rounds of gifts, and finally feasting. Marriages are usually arranged. However, modern brides and grooms have a greater say in whom they marry. Traditional weddings continue for three days. On the last day at the groom's ger, a family representative assures the bride's relatives that she will be safe. Then he offers a final toast before sending the guests home.

A wedding party

FOODS AND HOSPITALITY

Many unwritten laws of hospitality developed over the years due to huge distances between people on the steppe. Traditional etiquette for host and guest involved food, drink, and a bed for the night—even when the two were strangers. The same rules guide steppe dwellers today. Mongols treat strangers as if they were long-time friends. According to a Mongolian proverb, "Happy is he who often has guests; cheerful is the home near which stand the horses of visitors."

The first refreshment offered to guests is tea. In summer, tea is flavored with butter, milk, and salt. In winter, hosts add roasted flour of millet or rice. Some form of "white milk," or dairy product, accompanies the tea as a symbol of sincere welcome. *Airag* is Mongolia's national drink. It is made of fermented mare's milk and tastes like bubbly buttermilk. When offered, a polite guest is expected to drink three bowls. Other forms of milk,

Mongolia's national drink, airag

cheeses, butter, sour cream, and yogurt are made of milk from horses, goats, yaks, camels, and cows. Milk is the basic ingredient for at least thirty Mongolian foods.

A meat course typically follows tea and milk. Because of the healthy supply of livestock, meat has always been the national cuisine. A Mongolian proverb assures, "Grass for beasts, meat for men." Meat or milk products are main ingredients in soups, dumplings, or mixed with grains and noodles. Potatoes, onions, and other vegetables and some fruits are recent additions to the Mongolian diet.

Hosts pay special honors to guests by serving particular cuts of meat accompanied by warm milk wine. Hand gestures for serving and accepting dishes express respect and gratitude. Guests pour their wine from the silver *piala* set on a light-blue silk scarf. Then they offer good wishes to hosts in verse. Everyone at the table replies with, "May your good wishes come true!" Mongolian hospitality is as generous as the vast steppe.

*Visitors are very welcome
in Mongolia. Left: A stranger
is offered tea in a ger.
Below: A boat takes tourists
on Lake Khubsugul.*

Chapter 8

A VISIT INTO THE PAST AND THE FUTURE

TOURISM

Warm hospitality, endless natural beauty, interesting culture—
these are the features that attract visitors to Mongolia. Long ago,
foreign countries sent missionaries to bring back tales of this
unusual land. Isolation from the world during colonial periods
only increased interest in the curious, free-spirited people who
lived there. Today, the Mongolian People's Republic encourages
vacationers. The national tourist organization, Zhuulchin, reaches
out to foreign agencies worldwide. The government offers tours
for hunters, hikers, bird-watchers, mountain climbers, and
photographers. Guides cater to Russian, Polish, English, German,
French, Japanese, and Spanish groups. Tourism is a small but
growing industry in Mongolia's economy.

TOURIST CAMPS

Mongolia has three tourist camps in South Gobi, Khujirt, and
Terelj. Visitors live in gers and meet with local cattle-breeding
families. Each camp is centrally located for easy access to several

Above: Tortoise Rock
Right: The Orkhon River Valley

natural sights. They are in areas unspoiled by industry and city activity. Therefore, visitors experience the open yet lonely life of traditional nomads.

Khujirt lies near mineral hot springs in mid-Mongolia. The resort is a short distance from the thirteenth-century ruins of the ancient capital, Karakorum, and the original sixteenth-century Mongolian Buddhist temple of Erdene Zuu. Nearby is Orkhon waterfall, which formed after volcanic and earthquake activity some twenty-five thousand years ago.

Terelj is a mountain retreat just north of Ulan Bator. Many visitors call the camp a ''museum of natural wealth'' because of lush forests covering the lovely peaks. Wild animals, birds, and the famous Tortoise Rock formations draw visitors to this area. Terelj has local significance, too. Jugdermedidiyn Gurragcha, son of a herder, came from this village. He was the first Mongol to travel into space. Since orbiting the earth aboard the Soviet *Soyuz 39* in 1981, he has been a national hero.

An ibex

South Gobi is in south-central Mongolia at the base of the Altai Mountains. This desert camp seems more isolated than other tourist spots. However, primitive rock drawings give the impression that the Gobi has always been inhabited. Highlights of the region are preserved dinosaur skeletons with fossilized eggs. Tourists hike over sand dunes or picnic in mountain parks filled with wild horses, camels, snow leopards, mountain sheep, and gazelles. This camp is particularly popular with hunters. They come from Japan, the United States, and other countries and pay up to $16,000 for a packaged tour that includes a guide, cook, jeep and driver, and permission to hunt ibex and wild sheep.

CAPITAL CITY

Ulan Bator is Mongolia's political, economic, and cultural center. The 350-year-old city stretches along the Tul Riverbed

A modern section of Ulan Bator

with Mount Bogdo-ula, the world's oldest wildlife preserve, towering to the south. By Western standards, Ulan Bator is a fairly modern city. At one end of town is a string of smokestacks and many large factories. Two-thirds of the city's 550,000 people live in attractive three to six-story apartment buildings. At the other end of town, one-third of the population live in traditional felt tents that are fixed to the ground and hidden behind fences. Each year, new housing developments push the shrinking "city of felt" farther into the countryside.

Ulan Bator is Mongolia's capital and its first planned city. At independence, Ulan Bator was merely a collection of adobe monasteries and a sprinkling of gers. A twenty-year development program arranged for division of the city into nineteen *rayons,* or administrative subdivisions. Quality and beauty of streets, squares, and landscape governed city planning decisions.

The crowded section of Ulan Bator (left) is called "city of felt." Above: The museum of history

Each rayon now has a mixture of high-rise and apartment buildings served by their own cultural and public services. Stores, theaters, schools, national health-care services, restaurants, and government offices complete the neighborhoods. In the 1970s and 1980s many of the complexes resulted from Soviet loans. These areas are often referred to as "Brezhnev's Gifts," after the Soviet party leader during that time.

Other sights reflect Mongolia's affection for its neighbor to the north. The capital's main thoroughfare is named Lenin Prospect after the Russian revolutionary hero. And the slopes of the Khentai Mountains to the north are home to one of Ulan Bator's most imposing monuments, a heroic sculpture of a Russian soldier. The stone memorial serves as a reminder of the Soviet troops who helped Mongols drive the Japanese away in 1939.

Mongolia's greatest monument is the stone figure of Sukhe

101

Above: The Government Conference Center has some Mongolian-style architectural features in its modern facade. Right: Workers in a shoe factory

Bator, the national hero and party founder. The statue stands on the center square that bears his name. Government functions out of the white-marble-columned capitol building that shares the square. Here is where the Great Khural meets to make Mongolian policy.

More than ever, Ulan Bator reflects Mongolia's combined thrusts toward modernization and historic revival. Recently, city developers added a knit-clothing factory, tannery, and bakery. Ulan Bator has 240 major industrial programs representing one-third of the country's production. Young men and women wishing to trade their nomadic life-style for factory jobs flock to Ulan Bator. Women, in particular, find manufacturing to be a way out of traditional ger life. In some factories up to 80 percent of the workers are women. Women also represent about 50 percent of students enrolled in universities. With all of Mongolia's major research and university centers, the city is the country's economic and scientific capital as well.

Ulan Bator

Above: The monument of Sukhe Bator stands in Sukhe Bator Square in front of the capitol building. Below: The central library in Ulan Bator

Ulan Bator has many buildings dedicated to the arts and education.
The opera house (above), an exhibition building (below left),
and the theater of drama (below right) are some of them.

Bogdo Genen Palace in Ulan Bator, in Chinese-style architecture, is the former palace of the grand lama of Mongolia. Now it is the National Museum.

Similarly, the government commissions scores of cultural projects that begin in the capital. Ulan Bator boasts most of Mongolia's museums. They take visitors from ancient times through modern Mongolia. The State Central Museum features Mongolia's natural wealth and history. Exhibits depict early culture and customs. Displays of dress, household utensils, and work tools show different Mongolian nationalities. The Lenin Museum and Museum of the Revolution offer greater understanding of how modern Mongolia developed. At the Museum of the Revolution, displays concentrate on history of the people's struggle for independence and progress through socialism. From here, the Lenin Museum reveals how the revolution has been carried out in Mongolian life-style, art, and literature. Mongols value their museums as a way to tell about their land. Museums celebrating progress since revolution are part of every aimak. Mongols have an old proverb that says, "It is better to see than to hear."

DARKHAN

Darkhan is Mongolia's second major city and its first planned industrial center. In 1961, the government decided to construct a center devoted to mining and power for industry. The site chosen for the center was near a railway station between Ulan Bator and the Soviet border. The location was on main roads, and it had considerable water and mineral resources to handle growing industry. Additionally, the area had enough free land for building homes, utilities, and factories. Darkhan was a major step toward replacing Mongolia's nomadic society with a totally urban center. Even the name *Darkhan*, which means "blacksmith," symbolizes Mongolia's emphasis on its industrial future.

Within twenty years after the first cornerstone was laid, Darkhan's population grew from fifteen hundred to eighty-five thousand. The youthful city now boasts cement plants, brickworks, coal mines, power plants, and factories. Young Mongols wishing to make more money than they could earn on communes come looking for factory jobs that rival those in Ulan Bator. They travel along one of the few blacktop roads in Mongolia to get there. New apartment buildings, schools, hospitals, utilities, and landscaped squares are available to house the additional workers. Stores, cafes, restaurants, and movies help fill leisure time. Darkhan is still growing. Already the city is Mongolia's second industrial center.

ERDENET

Another city that grew from an industrial complex is Erdenet. Erdenet developed northwest of Ulan Bator. For centuries, herders who grazed livestock nearby believed that the mountain held great riches. In the 1960s, Mongolian and Czechoslovakian geologists unearthed large copper and molybdenum deposits. By the 1970s Soviets joined forces with Mongols to build processing plants for one of the richest deposits of these ores in the world.

Within a short time a cluster of gers was transformed into a modern town with a population of thirty thousand people. Large tracts of grazing land became self-contained town districts, drawing heat and power from nearby Darkhan and water from the Selenge River. High-rise flats and cultural and service centers outnumbered the single-story green and gray houses. Food, woodworking, and carpet industries developed. The goal was to have wives of miners become as famous for weaving ornate carpets as their husbands were for mining precious ore.

Specialists and workers from Soviet bloc countries contracted to work for an average of three years in Erdenet. Into the 1980s, about one-third of Erdenet workers were Soviets. Foreigners tended to group in separate sections of town with their own apartments, hospitals, schools, and social centers. As in other blossoming modern towns, the Soviets were helping Mongols build their future.

OTHER SETTLEMENTS

Many other settlements are villages and large camps by Western standards. For example, the agricultural cooperative in Bayandalay has rows of dreary one-story buildings facing an unpaved square. Although seemingly simple, the village contains a boarding school, hospital, library, and movie theater. The hope is that these areas will grow as more nomads settle.

Mongolians hope reform will allow them to gain greater prosperity and to build a new world without ignoring the old.

Mountains in the high plains tower over this nomad camp.

MONGOLIA'S FUTURE

Mongols agree that the time for change has come. However, they view reform as a path toward greater prosperity rather than an opportunity to wipe out the past. They want to build a new world with reminders of the old.

Today's Mongols are wealthier, healthier, and better educated than they were at the beginning of the revolution. These riches help reinforce modern Mongolia's strong sense of nationalism and deep pride in the past. At recent human rights demonstrations, banners read, "Mongolian brothers and sisters to your horses." The cry has been the same for ages. An old proverb says, "If a Mongol leaves his horse, he is no longer a Mongol." Only time will tell whether the government can settle all nomads and bring Mongolia into the twenty-first century.

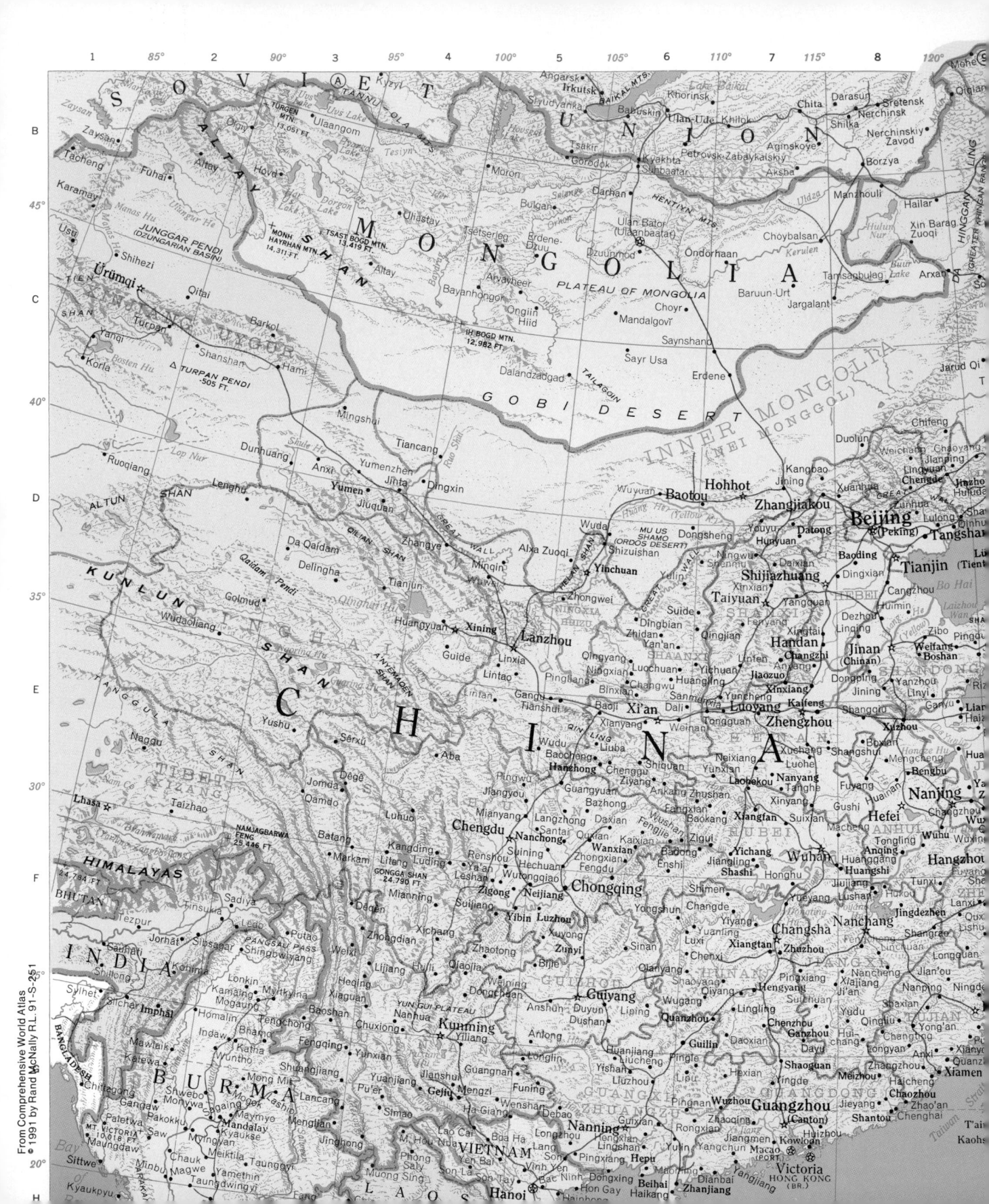

MAP KEY

Altay	B4
Arvayheer	B5
Baruun Urt	B7
Bayanhongor	B5
Bulgan	B5
Choybalsan	B7
Choyr	B6
Dalandzadgad	C5
Darhan	B6
Dzuunmod	B6
Erdene	C7
Erdene Dzuu	B5
Gorodok	A5
Hovd	B3
Jargalant	B8
Kyakhta	A6
Manalgovi	B6
Moron	B5
Olgiy	B2
Ondörhaan	B7
Ongiin Hiid	B5
Saynshand	C7
Sayr Usa	C6
Suhbaatar	A6
Tamsagbulag	B8
Tsakir	A5
Tsetserleg	B5
Ulaangom	B3
Ulan Bator (Ulaanbaatar)	B6
Uliastay	B4

MINI-FACTS AT A GLANCE

GENERAL INFORMATION

Official Name: Bügd Nayramdah Mongol Ard Uls (Mongolian People's Republic)

Government: Mongolia is changing its government from a Communist state with a highly centralized administration to a nation state with a multiparty political system. It is a unitary multiparty republic with two legislative houses. Legislative power rests with the popularly elected People's Great Khural (National Assembly). The Khural elects a ten-member Presidium, which holds the real executive power. Its chairman, the president, is also the head of state. The judicial system is a blend of Soviet, Chinese, and Turkish systems of law. Members of the Supreme Court are elected by the People's Great Khural. Mongolia does not accept International Court of Justice jurisdiction. The Mongolian People's Revolutionary party (Communist) is currently the major political party. All citizens over the age of 18 can vote. The capital is Ulan Bator.

Ethnic Composition: About 90% of the population is of Mongolian stock. Khalkha Mongols account for almost 75% of the Mongol group, and Buryat, Kazakhs, Khotons, Oirats, Tungus, and Tuvinians make up the rest. Non-Mongol groups are either Russians or Chinese.

Language: Khalkha Mongolian is the official language. Russian, Chinese, and English are spoken by minorities.

National Flag: Adopted in 1946, the Mongolian flag has three vertical bands of red, sky blue, and red. On the left red band a golden five-pointed star is placed and underneath, the golden *soyombo* (a combination of abstract devices) are arranged.

Coat of Arms: The wheat and cogwheel represent agriculture and industry. They are linked by a ribbon bearing the initials of the state name at the bottom and a five-pointed star at the top. Landscape inside the ribbon shows desert, steppe, and forest regions of Mongolia. The horseman racing into the sun stands for the nation's advance toward modern development.

National Anthem: "Bügd Nayramdah Mongol and ulsyn töriin duulal" ("State Anthem of the Mongolian People's Republic")

Membership in International Organizations: Mongolia is a member of the United Nations and some of its specialized agencies, Council for Mutual Economic Assistance (CEMA), and the Economic and Social Commission for Asia and the Pacific (ESCAP).

Money: The national currency is the tughrik, which is divided into 100 mongos. In 1992 one tughrik was equal to $.0235 in US currency.

Weights and Measures: The metric system is in use.

Population: 12,116,000 (1990 estimate); 3.5 persons per sq. mi. (1.4 persons per sq km); 53% urban and 47% rural

Religion: There is no state religion. Freedom of worship is guaranteed in the constitution, and all traditional religious practices, such as Lamaistic Buddhism, Shamanism, Islam, Christianity, and others are being given greater freedom to practice their faiths than under the old Communist government. Tibetan Buddhist Lamaism was the dominant religion in Mongolia for centuries.

Administrative Divisions: Mongolia is divided into 18 *aimaks* (provinces) and three autonomous municipalities of Ulan Bator, Darkhan, and Erdenet. Provinces are subdivided into 258 *somon*.

Area: 604,250 sq. mi. (1,565,000 sq km)

Cities: (1989 estimates)
Ulan Bator. 548,400
Darkhan 85,800
Erdenet 56,100

Other towns are Bayandalay, Choibalsan, Hatgal, Hovd, Moron, Onan, and Turta.

GEOGRAPHY

Borders: The USSR is in the north and China in the east, west, and south.

Land: Mongolia is the largest landlocked country in the world. Most of the land is high with an average altitude of 5,200 ft. (1,580 m). The Khangai region in the north has vast mountain ranges, deep valleys, salt lakes, and high steppe. The Altai, the Khangai, and the Khentei mountains are in the north. The Gobi region in the south has sparse grasslands, and rocky and sandy desert. The Darganga area of the eastern tip of the country contains some 220 extinct volcanoes. The Orkhon Waterfall was formed after volcanic and earthquake activity twenty-five thousand years ago.

Highest Point: Nayramdal Uul at 14,350 ft. (4,374 m) in the north.

Rivers: Mongolia lies on a continental divide. Rivers in the north flow northward into the Arctic Ocean and those in the northeast drain into the Pacific Ocean. In the west and south, seasonal rivers either end in salt lakes or disappear into the sands of the desert. Selenge is Mongolia's greatest river, followed by Dzavhan, Hovd, Kerulen, Onon, and Orkhon.

Lakes: Mongolia has more than 3,000 lakes. The largest is Lake Uvs in the north. Other lakes (all in the north) are Lake Bayan, Lake Har Us, Lake Hyargas, Lake Khubsugul, and Lake Terhiyn Tsagaan.

Forests and Grasslands: Huge expanses of pasturelands are covered with grasses and several fodder plant species. In summer the steppe are carpeted with bright violet, blue, red, and yellow flowers. Some 10% of the land is forested, consisting of siberian larch, cedar, spruce, pine, fir, birch, aspen, and poplar trees. A rich diversity of plant and animal life exists on the forest-steppe zone. *Gi-gi-tsao* grass has many uses such as horse feed, rope, and basket weaving. True desert conditions with very sparse vegetation exist only in the southern Gobi.

Wildlife: Mountain parks in the South Gobi are filled with wild horses, camels, snow leopards, mountain sheep, and gazelles. The world's oldest wildlife preserve is at Mount Bogdo-ula, near Ulan Bator. Large tracts of land on mountain ranges function as national wildlife reservations. Hunting for Mongolian horse, wild camel, antelope, and deer is banned. Mink, sable, and foxes are raised on government breeding farms. The rich and diverse wildlife has attracted international attention and has commercial importance. Wildlife consists of lynx, maral (Asiatic red deer), elk, roe deer, musk deer, brown bear, marmot, snow leopards, wild boars, sheep, asses, horses, and camels. Rich birdlife includes larks, partridges, cranes, pheasants, bustards, falcons, geese, ducks, black vultures, gulls, pelicans, swans, snowy owl, golden eagle, and condor.

Climate: Mongolia has a marked continental climate with cold winters and cool and hot summers, low rainfall, and high variation in daily and annual temperatures. Ulan Bator receives only about 9 in. (23 cm) of rainfall annually. Clear sunny days range between 200 to 260 each year.

Greatest Distances: East to west: 1,500 mi. (2,414 km)
North to south: 790 mi. (1,271 km)

EVERYDAY LIFE

Health: Health-care facilities are free in Mongolia. Every cooperative has either a hospital or a first-aid station. Helicopters carry doctors to remote areas. The state also operates a network of sanitoriums and holiday rest homes. The ancient art of acupuncture is popular. In the early 1990s there were some 400 persons per physician and some 90 persons per hospital bed.

Education: Educational development has been regarded as one of the most important issues. Secular (nonreligious) education is emphasized by the government. Beginning at six years of age, most children attend school for at least 10 years. The Mongolian State University was founded in Ulan Bator in 1942. There are teacher-training colleges and several vocational schools that teach agriculture, medicine, animal husbandry, and economics. In 1921 there was one general school, but by 1990 there were about 710 primary and secondary schools, 30 vocational and teacher-training schools, and eight institutions of higher learning. The literacy rate in the early 1990s was almost 90%.

Holidays

New Year's Day, January 1
Women's Day, March 8
International Socialist Worker's Day, May 1,
People's Revolution Day, July 11
USSR's October Revolution Day, November 7

Movable holidays include Mongol New Year's Day in February or March.

Culture: The *Secret History* and the seventeenth-century *Altan Tobchi* ("The Golden Chronicle") are Mongolia's most famous written records. A stone figure of Sukhe Bator, in the central square of Ulan Bator, is perhaps Mongolia's greatest monument. Almost all cultural projects are commissioned by the government. The State Central Museum features Mongolia's natural wealth and history. The Lenin Museum and the Museum of the Revolution (1971) show the history of Mongolian development. The Palace Museum has a superb collection of folk art. The Religious Museum (1903-05) houses rare Buddhist relics. The State Public Library at Ulan Bator contains 3 million volumes of great variety and historical value. The State Drama Theater (1931) shows both Mongolian and classical work. The Mongolian National Orchestra performs Oriental and European music. Western rock music is also popular and is played by rock groups such as the Bayan Mongol Band.

Housing: Mongolian traditional housing reflects steppe life-style. The most common houses in the countryside and on state cooperative farms are the *gers* or *yurts*. These are portable tentlike houses that are made of heavy felt covering a circular wooden frame. Ropes made of grass secure the felt over the frame. The ger is arranged in a traditional fashion. There is a set place for furniture, bedding, guest seat, Buddha altar, and storage chests. Some modern appliances or furnishings, such as a sewing machine, radio, TV, and stoves are found in gers of some well-to-do Mongols. In cities gers have been replaced by four-story Soviet-style apartment buildings. There are also some permanent gers on the outskirts of cities.

Clothing: Both men and women wear the traditional *del*, a loose ankle-length robe with high collar and leather linings and boots to protect against frigid temperatures. Dels are adorned with brightly colored sashes. In cities, however, European clothing has largely replaced traditional dels.

Food: Mongolians are famous for their hospitality to their guests. Tea, sometimes flavored with butter, milk, and salt, is a popular refreshment drink. *Airag* (fermented mare's milk) is Mongolia's national drink. Cheese, butter, sour cream, and yogurt are made of milk from horses, goats, yaks, camels, and cows. The Mongolian diet consists mainly of milk and meat products used in soups, wine, dumplings, grains, and noodles. With the spread of agriculture, vegetables and fruits have become recent additions to the Mongolian diet. Fish and fish products are rarely eaten by Mongols.

Sports and Recreation: The Nadam Festival or "The Three Games of Men" is the most popular national sports event. It involves wrestling, archery, and horse racing. Wrestling is popular, and boys begin learning techniques at the age of eight or nine. Mongols also enjoy skiing, table tennis, volleyball, soccer, basketball, motorcycling, rifle shooting, boxing, and gymnastics. Playing of chess and checkers is a popular wintertime home activity. Folk dancing where men and women dance together in gaily colored costumes in small groups is very popular. The Mongolian circus is performed in a large ger with goats, yaks, and wolves along with the "rubber acrobats." *Zhuulchin*, the national tourist organization, offers tours for hunters, hikers, bird watchers, mountain climbers, and photographers. Mongolia has three established tourist camps in South Gobi, Khujirt, and Terelj.

ECONOMY AND INDUSTRY

Agriculture: Roughly 80% of the land is meadows and pastures, and less than 1% is under cultivation. The government is trying to encourage agriculture among nomadic Mongol herders. All agricultural areas are under state collective farms. Some large state farms average about 700 sq. mi. (1,813 sq km). With Soviet-supplied farm equipment and irrigation facilities, wheat, oats, barley, rye, hay, fruits, and vegetables are grown.

Livestock: Livestock raising is the mainstay of Mongolia's economy and commerce. Livestock population outnumbers people thirteen to one—the largest ratio in the world. Sheep, goats, cattle, horses, pigs, and camels are raised on the endless steppe. Some 14 million sheep make up 60% of the total livestock population. Cattle and wool make up some 75% of the country's total exports.

Fish: There are 70 freshwater species of fish including salmon, trout, grayling, perch, and whitefish. Fish is caught commercially for export, as there is hardly any local consumption.

Mining: One of the richest copper and molybdenum deposits in the world exist near Erdenet. Vast deposits of coal, iron, tin, gold, silver, fluorite, tungsten, petroleum, salt, shale, and fluorspar also exist.

Manufacturing: With Mongolia's enormous livestock population, most manufacturing is based on livestock by-products. Leather tanneries, shoe factories, wool and meat processing plants, garment knitting, and dairies are the chief manufacturing sectors. Other manufactured products include tent frames and felts, furniture, glass and china, soap, and matches. Pelts are made from fur-bearing animals like the marmot.

Transportation: Horses and camels provide excellent steppe transportation. The Trans-Mongolian Railway links Moscow in the north and Beijing in the south. The

Moscow-Ulan Bator-Beijing Express runs each way once a week. There are some 1,128 mi. (1,815 km) of railways, and about 30,600 mi. (49,200 km) of roads. Less than 2% of roads are paved, as most travel is over the dry, flat steppe. Trucks, buses, motorbikes, jeeps, and cars are common in cities. Mongolian Airline service connects Ulan Bator with other countries and provincial capitals. Special medical and veterinary flights also are arranged. Camels are still used to carry freight in the sparsely populated desert area of the south while yak and oxen haul goods in the rugged mountainous area in the west. The Selenge River and Lake Uvs are used for transporting goods to the USSR.

Communication: More than 70 newspapers and periodicals are published in Mongolian, Russian, English, French, Chinese, and Kazakh languages. *Unen* ("Truth") and *Pionyeriyn Unen* ("Pioneer's Truth") are the leading newspapers. In the early 1990s, there were 275,000 radios (one per 7 persons), 120,000 TV sets (one per 17 persons), and some 63,000 telephones (one per 35 persons).

Trade: Since Mongolia is a landlocked country, its imports and exports travel overland largely through the Soviet Union. The chief exports are live animals, and animal by-products such as meat, butter, wool, hair, hides, and fur, plus cement and lumber. Major imports are machinery, fuel, metals, chemicals, clothing, consumer goods, sugar, and fertilizers. Chief trading partners are the USSR and other Socialist countries.

IMPORTANT DATES

551-556 — Turks fight the Juan Empire; Bumin becomes the first Turkish emperor

1162 — Genghis Khan (Temujin) is born

1203 — A single Mongolian feudal state is formed under Genghis Khan

1206 — Genghis Khan assembles a great council *kuriltai* to choose one ruler over Asia

1220 — City of Karakorum is founded near Orhon Gol

1227 — Genghis Khan dies

1279 — Kublai Khan proclaims himself emperor of Mongolia and united China, and establishes the Yuan Dynasty

1281 — Kublai Khan's fleet is destroyed by devastating storms near Japanese coast

1294 — Kublai Khan dies

1368 — Mongol Dynasty in China is overthrown; Ming Dynasty is established

1571 — Altan Khan and China finalize a treaty ending border disputes

1644 — Manchus conquer China

1689 — Treaty of Nerchinsk is signed between Russia and China

1691 — Outer Mongolia comes under the Manchu rule and remains a Chinese province till 1911

1727 — Russia and China sign the Treaty of Kyakhta defining the border between China and Outer Mongolia that exists in large part today

1903-05 — The Temple of Generous Mercy, a Buddhist shrine, is built

1911 — Mongols proclaim their independence of Manchu rule

1912-19 — Outer Mongolia remains an autonomous state under Russian protection

1917 — Russian Revolution topples tsarist rule in Russia

1919-21 — Outer Mongolia once again becomes a Chinese province

1920 — The Living Buddha of Urga appeals to Soviet regime for aid to eliminate Chinese rule from Outer Mongolia; Mongolian Revolutionary Press issues the first issue of *Mongolyn Unen* ("Mongolian Truth")

1921 — Mongolian People's party under the leadership of Sukhe Bator is established; provisional People's Government declares independence of Mongolia; joint Mongol and Soviet forces occupy Urga; People's Revolutionary Government is established

1923 — Revolutionary leader Sukhe Bator dies

1924 — City of Urga renamed as Ulan Bator (Red Hero); first Mongolian stamp issued; name of party is changed to Mongolian People's Revolutionary party (MPRP); People's Great Khural meets for the first time, adopts a constitution, and under Premier Choibalsan proclaims the country independent

1925 — Soviet troops leave Mongolia; Mongolian currency, *tughrik*, is issued

1932 — Private industry is banned, government seizes hundreds of estates to promote collectives

1934 — Secret agreement is reached between USSR and Mongolia for mutual assistance in case of Japanese aggression

1935—Soviet troops reenter Mongolia to stop Japanese attacks along Manchurian border

1936—A formal 10-year USSR-Mongolia treaty of friendship and mutual defense is signed

1936-39—Choibalsan emerges as the party leader; widespread arrests of monastic leaders from religious institutions

1939—Peace is negotiated between USSR and Japan after large-scale fights take place on Mongolia-Manchuria border

1940—Choibalsan is comfirmed as party leader and a new constitution is adopted

1945—Mongolia declares war on Japan; Republic of China (Taiwan) agrees to recognize the independence of Outer Mongolia; Mongol people vote for independence from China in a plebiscite

1946—China recognizes Mongolia as an independent country; Mongolia and USSR sign another treaty of friendship and mutual assistance; Cyrillic alphabet is officially adopted for Mongolian language, with two extra symbols

1948-52—Mongolia's first five-year plan

1949—China and Mongolia establish diplomatic relations

1950—USSR and China sign treaty guaranteeing Mongolian independence

1952—Choibalsan dies; Yumjaagiin Tsedenbal becomes party and government leader

1953—The government of the Republic of China (Taiwan) abrogates its treaty with the USSR and nullifies its recognition of Mongolian independence

1953-57—Mongolia's second five-year plan

1955—Trans-Mongolian Railway, linking Moscow to Beijing, is completed

1958—Government begins a campaign to introduce collective animal husbandry and agriculture

1960—Mongolia and China sign a treaty of friendship and mutual assistance; the current constitution is adopted

1961—Mongolia admitted as a member of the United Nations

1961-65—Mongolia's third five-year plan

1962—Mongolia becomes member of Soviet-organized CEMA; border demarcation agreement signed with China

1964—Mongolia and USSR sign a 20-year treaty of friendship

1966-70—Mongolia's fourth five-year plan

1969—The term of the People's Great Khural is changed from 3 to 4 years

1971—The government permits the Gandan Monastery to reopen its religious school

1971-75—Mongolia's fifth five-year plan

1972—Japan and Mongolia agree to exchange diplomatic representation

1976—USSR and Mongolia sign a border treaty

1976-80—Mongolia's sixth five-year plan

1977—Japan and Mongolia sign an economic cooperation treaty; former East Germany and Mongolia sign treaty of friendship and cooperation; Algeria and Mongolia sign a treaty of cultural and scientific cooperation; Hungary and Mongolia sign agreement about dual citizenship

1978—Laos and Mongolia sign agreement on economic cooperation; North Korea and Mongolia revise cooperative programs

1981—The first Mongol goes into space aboard Soviet *Soyuz 39*

1981-85—Mongolia's seventh five-year plan

1983—Mongolia expels some 7,000 ethnic Chinese

1986—General elections take place

1987—Soviet Union announces the removal of an armored division and small units of Soviet army from Mongolia; Mongolia and the US establish diplomatic relations

1988—Second Mongol-American Bilateral Conference is held in Ulan Bator; a border treaty is signed with China; Mongolian Democratic Union party is founded

1989—A population census is taken; Mongolian foreign minister pays China a visit—the first in 40 years

1990—The statue of Stalin in central Ulan Bator is removed by popular demand; People's Great Khural legalizes political parties; the first multiparty general elections are held; Mongolian people oppose close Soviet relations; 70 out of some 500 Buddhist monasteries are reopened

1991—US President George Bush grants Mongolia most-favored-nation trade status

IMPORTANT PEOPLE

Roy Chapman Andrews (1884-1960), American zoologist and explorer who led expeditions into the Gobi in the 1920s and 1930s

Sukhe Bator (1894-1923), Mongolia's greatest hero, who founded the Mongolian People's Republican party and the modern Mongolian state

Khorloghiyin Choibalsan (1895-1952), Mongolian national leader

Tsendyn Damdinsuren (1908-   ) one of the most important Mongolian modern writers

Jugdermedidiyn Gurragcha (1947-   ), son of a Mongol herder, he was the first Mongol to travel into space aboard the Soviet *Soyuz 39*, in 1981

Nyamyn Jamba, famous Mongolian sculptor who carved statues of Mongolian heroes

Genghis Khan (1162-1227), the most famous of the khans, set up the first Mongolian empire in 1206

Kublai Khan (1216-94), Mongol empire's most famous emperor, who conquered most of China

Timur Lenk or Tamer Lane (1336?-1405), a descendant of Genghis Khan, he extended his military power to southern Russia and India

Ch. Lodoydamba (1917-70), Mongolian composer of music

Dashdorjiin Natsaghdorj (1906-37), famous Mongolian author, acclaimed as founder of modern Mongolian literature. His most famous poem is "My Homeland."

Ogodei (1185-1241), Genghis Khan's third son, who became emperor after Genghis Khan

Ch. Oydov (1917-63), Mongolian playwright

E. Oyuun (1908-   ), Mongolian playwright

Marco Polo (1254-1324), a Venetian visitor who wrote *Description of the World*, giving an account of his 17-year stay during the Yuan Dynasty

B. Rindhen (1905-78), Mongolian writer

Toulun (A.D. 500), famous Juan leader who drove competing tribes westward to the Caspian Sea

Yumjaagiin Tsedenbal (1916-   ), general secretary of the Central Committee for many years

INDEX

Page numbers that appear in boldface type indicate illustrations

About the Author

Marlene Targ Brill is a free-lance Chicago-area writer, specializing in fiction and nonfiction books, articles, media, and other educational materials for children and adults. Among her credits are *John Adams* and *I Can Be a Lawyer* for Childrens Press; *Washington, D.C. Travel Guide*, a regular column for the secondary publication, *Career World;* and contributions to World Book Encyclopedia's *The President's World* and *Encyclopaedia Britannica.*

Ms. Brill holds a B.A. in special education from the University of Illinois and an M.A. in early childhood education from Roosevelt University. She currently writes for business, health care, and young people's publications and is active in Chicago Women in Publishing and Independent Writers of Chicago.

Ms. Brill has written *Libya* and *Algeria* in the Enchantment of the World series. She would like to acknowledge the encouragement of her husband, Richard, and daughter, Alison—two people who particularly crave knowledge and appreciate a good book.